BOOKS & CHAPBOOKS BY AARON SHURIN

Black Roses

The Blue Absolute

Flowers & Sky: Two Talks

The Skin of Meaning: Collected Literary Essays and Talks

Citizen

King of Shadows

Threshold (with Helen Douglas)

Involuntary Lyrics

Three Scenes from the Sauna at the YMCA

A Door

The Paradise of Forms: Selected Poems

Unbound: A Book of AIDS

Codex

Four Views Out of Paris

Into Distances

Narrativity

A's Dream

Elsewhere

The Graces

Giving up the Ghost

Toot Suite

The Night Sun

Woman on Fire

ELIXIR

NEW & SELECTED POEMS

Elixir

AARON SHURIN

NEW & SELECTED POEMS

NIGHTBOAT BOOKS
NEW YORK

Printed in the United States

ISBN: 978-1-643-62276-7

"The Story I Tell" and "Memorial Day" were first published in *Poetry*.

"City of Men," "A's Dream," "Material's Daughter," "Elsewhere," and "All That" were originally published in *A's Dream* (O Books, 1989, second printing, 2010). Reprinted with permission of the author and the Estate of Leslie Scalapino (O Books).

Design and composition by Kit Schluter
Typeset in Baskerville and ACADEMY ENGRAVED LET

Cover art: "Covered Goblet with a Winged Ball on Top" by Albrecht Altdorfer, ca. 1520-1525, Etching, Rosenwald Collection, The National Gallery of Art, Washington D.C.

Cataloging-in-publication data is available from the Library of Congress

Nightboat Books
New York
www.nightboat.org

CONTENTS

NEW POEMS

BLACK ROSES

from A DOOR (2000)

from INVOLUNTARY LYRICS (2005)

from CITIZEN (2012)

ELIXIR

NEW & SELECTED POEMS

HELPLESS BEFORE DESIRE

A FOREWORD

ABOUT halfway through this book, just over two decades into Aaron Shurin's five-decade career, you'll find "Human Immune," a prose poem the *San Francisco Chronicle* once called "an unflinching masterpiece." I read it as central to Shurin's oeuvre, a triumphal mid-career pivot between the earlier mastery of *A's Dream* and the later masteries of *Involuntary Lyrics* and the recent sequence "Black Roses." Given its publication history, Shurin must have felt from the start how pivotal "Human Immune" was. He first collected it in 1997's hybrid-genre *Unbound: A Book of AIDS*, and reissued it twice in close succession, first in 1999's *The Paradise of Forms: Selected Poems* and then in 2000's *A Door*, his sixth full-length book of poems. Published just five years after the first protease inhibitors changed the prognosis for HIV infection, *A Door* was the first book of Shurin's I read, and "Human Immune" broke me open.

I didn't understand it at first. Its sentences bypassed conventional grammar to speak directly to embodied knowledge of the AIDS crisis, which was, though I could not yet know it, already becoming historical. And despite the decades that have since passed, this poem remains for me an open portal to eros; its syntax carries the power of the erotic to change, with its galvanic charge, both experience and our language for it. "I lie in your arms. I kiss your mouth," the poem begins, "Use your nails, creature." "Helpless before desire," the speaker of "Human Immune" professes opulent appetite undiminished by HIV/AIDS: "I have to get my hands on the world," he confesses. In fact, his commitment to eros has perhaps become more heightened, a site of queer resistance by virtue of its insistence on his—our—aliveness. It was a time when so many of us had died.

"Dead from complicity in San Francisco discharged me, the harp of a person had an arc," he writes at the start of the poem's second verse paragraph. The sentence bristles, agitating against complicity, and exemplifies how, even in extremis, Shurin allows prosody to do its work. The alliteration and slant rhymes of complicity/discharged me and discharged/harp/arc musically fuse together the sentence's two halves, the first of which delivers a sharp rhetorical point and the second of which never ceases to astonish me. It was impossible at the time not to read "arc" also as "A.R.C.," acronym for AIDS-related Complex, dreaded because the cluster of infections it indicated was so often terminal. There was something magical, inexplicable, transformative, and healing in that complex intersection of musical instrument, personhood, shape, and disease—and there still is.

I didn't know how badly I needed Shurin's poem before I read it, in large part because I'd never before read a poem that captured how the gay body politic, gay sex, and the surreality of AIDS body horror informed and at times became conflated with each other. "The face ripping wide open has led a team of men in white gowns and slow rhythm," he writes, and soon after, "On his back at the edge of the couch to die of pleasure, kneeling into your asshole to form around me." Images of bodily dissolution, medicalization, and erotic encounter mix throughout the poem, which captures the fact that it was no simple thing to remain open to eros in the context of AIDS. "A cure may be possible — tell me what words mean," he writes plaintively, before commanding "Pleasure for a coffin: turn and enter your home." Note the jump-cut from hope to hopelessness, the subsequent turn from uncertainty to certainty: they render with precision the existential flailing characteristic of that traumatic time like few other texts I know.

But Shurin's lyric sensibility, whether rendered in lines or in sentences, has always been sensitive and attuned to our historical weathers, and his career spans Gay Liberation, the AIDS crisis, and the subsequent enfranchising of queer people and putative "mainstreaming" of our culture. It's one of the attendant pleasures of *Elixir*'s robust selection of poems: book in hand, you can track these shifts to a degree. Shurin's early Gay Lib volumes, *The Night Sun* and *Giving up the Ghost*, "speak of ourselves . . . beyond the stern/and arrogant borders of manhood," while *A's Dream* takes us on what Shurin calls "an erotic rampage" by collaging Whitman's pastoral landscapes with San Francisco's "City of Men." We segue from Gay Liberation's iconic literary ancestor to the AIDS-era volumes *Unbound* and *A Door*. Later we immerse ourselves in *Involuntary Lyrics*, an ingeniously designed formal queering of Shakespeare's sonnets that refuses to make our desires less radical. If anything, his angular American sonnets are "a wake-up call: increase/energy, attention."

Himself awakened by '60s and '70s countercultures, Shurin learned early to make poems that channel liberatory energies. After receiving his BA from University of California-Berkeley, where he studied with Denise Levertov, Shurin decamped to the Boston area, then home to *Fag Rag* and some of the country's most radical Gay Liberation activists. He stayed for five years, during which he helped found the Good

Gay Poets collective. After returning to the Bay, he published his first book with Gay Sunshine Press in San Francisco, beginning a lifelong pattern of working with small presses on the vanguard of queer and literary publishing. He went on to publish with some of the great gay editors of the late 20th and early 21st centuries, issuing *The Graces* with Donald Allen at Four Seasons, *Into Distances* and *Unbound* with Douglas Messerli at Sun & Moon, *The Paradise of Forms* and *A Door* with Ed Foster at Talisman House, and *The Blue Absolute* and now *Elixir* with Stephen Motika at Nightboat Books. Along the way he also collaborated with small presses central to the Bay Area's aesthetic independence: *A's Dream* with O Books, *Involuntary Lyrics* with Omnidawn, and *Citizen* with the legendary City Lights.

This publication history underscores the fact that Shurin is a peerless syncretist, integrating aspects of Gay Liberation, Black Mountain, New York School, Language, and New Narrative poetics. As documented in the essential essays and talks in *The Skin of Meaning*, his Romantic ancestors are Whitman and Dickinson; his Modernist ancestors include Baudelaire, H. D., Woolf, Proust, and Colette; his elders are Levertov, Robert Duncan, and Diane DiPrima; and his compatriots include Norma Cole, Robert Glück, David Melnick, Alice Notley, Michael Palmer, and Leslie Scalapino. And like Scalapino especially, Shurin has participated in and contributed to Bay Area poetry community without sounding remotely like anyone else. As paratactic as Ron Silliman, as lyric as Duncan, as frankly gay as Glück, Shurin's verse and prose poems say YES to the pleasures of disjunction, high song, and the queerly fabulous. Gestural and intense, they enact a lyric paradox: grounded in the social, they move toward transcendence. As he explains in his iconic talk "Narrativity:"

> One seeks to be out of order, to shiver out of subjectivity, to shake off the mask of the material *and* to shimmy in its arms, to finally retreat from logic and advance by radial maneuvers, gathering meaning.

Like Duncan before him, Shurin has remained fiercely loyal to San Francisco, and like Duncan's, his poems are not merely parochial. Their radical "radial maneuvers" were made possible by his education in the Poetics Program at New College and the cross-fertilization of the Bay Area poetry scene when it was still both highly diverse and contentious, litigating itself in the pages of *Poetry Flash* and small lit mags as well as through talk and reading series. During and after the Poetry Wars, Shurin has kept alive the legacies of Duncan and the Poetics Program through talks, essays, and teaching. That's how I first came to know him in person, as co-founder and co-director of the MFA program at the University of San Francisco; later, I would teach poetry workshops and poetics seminars there, and in doing so, witness firsthand the way his curriculum fostered fierce attention to syllable, pulse, sound, and line, while also encouraging expansive conceptualizing of poetry's aesthetic and political possibilities.

Inseparable from his long residence in San Francisco, Shurin and his work have long done their part in furthering what the city has made possible for queer lives and art. Only one among many who have studied his poems and poetics and learned from his curricula, I would not be the poet, thinker, and teacher I am without his example. I moved to the Bay in 2000 and read *A Door* soon after I arrived. It elicited the earliest inklings that I belonged there, and the chance acquisition of Shurin's Sun & Moon chapbook *Narrativity* spurred me to write my first poetics essay: "Aaron Shurin's *A Door*—On the Embodied Lyric." Unsure whether it was any good, I shared a draft with a friend;

somehow the draft found its way to Norma Cole, who sent it to Shurin, who summoned me via email to his office at USF on Lone Mountain. That's where we first met, and how I learned that since the late '80s he'd been generating his poems procedurally.

I experienced *A Door* as a somatic event before my mind reached toward the book's semantic sense. Even after I began to parse it more logically, it struck me as staunchly embodied, each pulse and vowel of its sentences an extension of fleshy sentience. In my essay, I described it as "a lyric fabric whose structuring principle is body logic, an erotic rubric where the mind is loosed, fluid, and mutable among the physical." Sitting in Shurin's office I began to see how procedure—which I had associated with a cold Conceptualism—could engender that queer feeling of embodied prosody. Shurin's almost divinatory compositional process actually allowed mind to be "loosed, fluid, and mutable among the physical," especially since he was more or less bibliomantic, never as rigid as other proceduralists. Working with a small archive of books per poem, he established nonce rules to help him select one word at a time (even articles!), moving from book to book in sequence. Procedure, as he says in an interview with Lily Iona MacKenzie, simply procured "the words to compose as I needed." Varying the constraints from poem to poem, he wrote steadily through the decades from 1989's *A's Dream* to 2020's *The Blue Absolute*. And though Shurin no longer generates poems through procedure, the long practice of doing so has left him with an unbreakable fluency and the undimmed facility to compose as he needs.

Throughout this foreword I've foregrounded some historical, political, and material contexts for Shurin's work and career. And though that seems to me a fitting approach to a career retrospective, I want to acknowledge it might not jibe with Shurin's own sense of how best to approach his work. Raving, raging, grieving, and loving, Shurin's work has always been ecstatic, both in the Romantic sense of aesthetic or erotic rapture and in the more ancient metaphysical sense of a withdrawal of the soul from the body in a trance. As the title *Elixir* suggests, Shurin's poems can suggest the occult and the curative, whether by enacting a Gay Liberation ritual to exorcise "the straight/man/demon" or by concocting a tonic for a body politic fevered by AIDS. My own initial experience of *A Door* as somatic suggests that his poems can in fact be taken as draughts, potent antidotes to logical thought.

Rooted in the Arabic, *al-iksir*, for a miraculous medicine, elixir indicates, on the literal level, "a strong extract," and on the figurative level, "the quintessence of a thing," all of which are true of this selection of poems. The *Elixir* you're holding is the precious decoction of a life's work, a combination of distilled essences found nowhere else in American poetry. Shurin long ago perfected the "floating perfumes and delirium" of this singular poetics—I almost wrote *potion*—and its heady signature effects have only gained in potency with each passing decade. With this elixir, Shurin promises in an essay on his prosody, "the poem falls more in love with meaning" and "writer and reader are drawn into the embrace." If it had a color, it might be absinthe but iridescent, the kind of green you'd see as sheen on a beetle's back. If it had a taste, perhaps it would be as sweetbitter as Sappho's wild apple, nearly ripe and still unpicked on the topmost branch. To ingest any elixir begets a drama of promise and anticipation. Drink up, reader. Touch what happens next.

—BRIAN TEARE

NEW POEMS

THE STORY I TELL

The gates, the gardens, the windows, the sky, the ledge of bricks, the fallen leaves, the porch where I kissed you long ago, the name you unraveled inside my head, the piece of a body stuck to the wall, the ticking clock that caught in your teeth, I read a book, I take a walk, I swallow the sky of here and now, I shake my pockets to hear my coins, I move the table from here to there, I struggle to struggle with honor and truth, I remember the hair that stuck to your lips, I taste your lips with the hair on my tongue, I whistle alone when the light is dim, the stove, the sofa, the creaky door, the bed, the blanket, the common bonds, the morning rays, the salty skin, the story I tell of the story we made, September, October, November . . .

MEMORIAL DAY

And still one looks to the tree to paraphrase the sky, arbiter of wind and sun. The hills with their cross-hatch houses and vertical streets . . . You gave an impassioned speech to the pigeons, who lifted, as if with one wing, into a wheeling arc: hiss of the air streaming through their gray feathers; it sounded like kiss me or kill me I couldn't tell.

This is the life of your time. Look the clouds puff and streak as a gesture of faith. You are written and erased

POETICS

Was it the blue cloud of his mind? Was it the sun of her brain? Here is the wind of their eyes. There is the rain of my hope. Is it a language of sighs, a brawl of interjections, of grammatical contraptions and syntactic obfuscations, there is the tiny planet in transit from east to west, is it,? from left to right? There are the ravens squawking in sidereal tempo, or a picture-book of samurai erections, he shakes his head to parse the impressions of living authoritative spark plugs and guarded nations, is it a language of closure or rebirth, arbitrary sensations, or have they mastered the form of incarnation: the dog with a human face or the girl with an elephant trunk? The girl with an elephant trunk walks into a bar, etc. . . . Is it the shame of novelty or the rigor of attention, whose hand, whose tooth, whose book, whose cloud whose sun whose rain whose sighs . . . ?

AND WHAT

Where is the emergency room for your spirit, for your courage, for your artisan eye or alphabetic zeal? Where is your cloudless sky? She thumbs through the questions as her cheeks flush and a nervous twitch appears in her right eye. And what she thought, and what she wondered and wanted and who she thought she was . . . Life gives its soul to death, she thought, in symbiotic amplitude, and I'm stuck with both. There are deficiencies, additions, enumerations, and elaborations—perpetual translation—of matter and what's the matter, the questions fired at her head by her head, and that little girl in a starched pink dress dragging her stuffed monkey in the dirt by its tail—excreting the past—of which she can't stop talking, as who she was who she became she is, narrating the decade the epoch the day to expiate the decade the epoch the day as if pages torn from a book and nothing done, nothing projected—at last, she thought, finally—reciting her favorite poem and let it hang in the air—   *vaporously*   *the unmoving*   *blue* . . .

THE NATURALIST

What do we see first when we open our eyes? The billowing curtain, blue turned to lavender under the sun's breath. We hear the toot of the tugboat, a little pig in the water. If you have a place to go to go now. Slaughter in the plaza, we speak in hushed tones dismembering the lumbering past. What is a coin really made of? Coiled energy? Suspended sweat? A discrete promise of redemption? If you have a place to come from come now. We think of a thing that we want and it becomes a golden pellet. I watch the afternoon fog overtake the hills, a total disappearing act, but the morning fog vanishes from within, invisible dissolution, an exhale. Are the clouds and the sky and the molecules of water actually breathing in and out? The lungs of the spewing volcano, the suction of the spinning tornado, the roiling typhoon inhaling the coconut palms . . . If you have a heaven to rise to rise now . . .

DOME

What of other dimensions in the dome of space? What if he can't see, can't smell, can't touch the living parts, a city spectral, psychedelic, a city unknown? What if some alien spore comes and steals his cobalt eyes . . . ? From his hospital bed in

the repurposed truck he imagines the chug of the engine as it drags me through time, my throat strafed and my lungs befouled—to chart the distance between the city of breath and the city of dust—and try my hand at making a world . . . The night translucent

for dark things. I roll in my bed as if surfing the flooded, empty streets, the boarded-up shops, the closed cafés with their handmade signs pleading "health and good fortune" and "we miss your lungs"—as the city gasps for air . . . Once I stood upright

and scanned the horizon for meat. Once we stayed in bed forever in the electric night—socket and plug—for a long jolt of wishful thinking as the current sputtered and the lights cut out. Is that thing the sky now: blue venom? Does it render our chests

useless, heaving like sea swells in a teacup, stinging like smoke? He stands on a quiet corner in a patch of pale light they used to call sun with no cars gunning and no walkers loosening their legs. Struck dumb by the speed with which silence descended

he coughs up a worm or two, ponders the sinking ground . . . If he sips gray water from his catgut bag, is that a vision quest? He sees what he wants to see, is that 20-20 eyesight for real? You made a world and spun it on your finger, you made the people

with their drooping necks and bulging eyes; their hunger unslaked . . . You made what you needed to see and yes my body is falling away, I'm just a passenger now, not detached but watching: the unspooling, the cut threads, foot, tooth, shoulder—

You lean into the storm of changes as your body releases its coils and springs—stiff where you used to swivel, commander of action, ideation, recitation—faltering now in the cataleptic swell of constant erasure. Words spread their wings,

take flight into the diaspora of signs where the lost nouns gather, memories jostle for rank and place, and your unfinished quest—I was here, I am here—hovers like a charm of hummingbirds: the living apparatus of suspended animation.

I let go to feel the lift—levitation is my exodus—imagine the future as "up" and the past as "below." There's an equanimity to floating, a balance of forces rising and falling. I close my eyes: nothing . . . It's everything I needed to be . . .

THE INCARNATE

In the middle, not the beginning or the end—a thunder-clap that has him fleeing the house (how else would the jungle prevail?)—running to keep up with the past—then let him wrestle the lightning. She, on the other hand, knits her sweaters and hats—magnetic loops—you start with a plug of yarn and believe in the future. Are you patient? Have you scoured the calendar, the barometer, the odometer, the alarm clock, and the tides? You can hear the screech of the opening door, prelude to the boom and the bang, feel the pull on the solar plexus, urging you back to the human delegation, with your teeth crooked or missing, and a runaway gland in your neck. I watch your ambivalence—the body is made for living not dying—as you nod your head up and down, left to right, to accommodate the shifting persuasions. You are my brother, my other, my another. We lie down together in the dusk of December and breathe . . .

A FINAL ADDRESS TO THE JURY

I don't want any of that, not of him doing this or her doing that . . . I want miasma, an undifferentiated mass of cells, a blob of intent sweeping down the street. Strollers pass but I narrow my eyes to fudge their features. I don't want to see a "man" or a "woman"—nothing gendered, nothing aged—not a person or a place—just sheer movement, as if the stream of fog had stripped the walkers of their hats and shoes, of their shirts and shorts, of their bodies and blood. I don't want to be judged *or* appreciated; I was galactic, born among stars; I studied the coordinates of the space telescope's astounding pictures to locate my home. It's been lovely since I dropped my face and form. I'm pure feeling, in relation to nothing. I'm embedded in the universe as a construct, written by shadows and light, by gravity and magnetism, by axis and tilt. I'm at peace in my sky up there. *"I depart as air."*

A VIEW FROM THE YARD

Little pop-stars on the Jasmine bush—sniff. What the sun does to a cold mind: I forget the emotional litigations, the character assassinations, the fanatical condemnations; I block out your plea-bargain eyes . . . It's sunny and green in my new backyard, by the big yucca's bulging trunk, biomorphic, an elephant, a mastodon. I can no longer remember the delicacies of the flesh but I can still taste them on my tongue. Abolition of sentiment, to keep the channels clear—Light wind and quick slashes of sun—It's spring so the clams are wriggling in their shells, the shells are glistening on the bank, a family drags their baskets across the sand, shamed by the iridescence of the sea. I can't shake the look on their fallen faces, like a rejected limb—The inundation of blossoms and buds in the air—I don't remember the person who birthed me but I can't forget the one who kicked me out the door, what Paradise! I recall a lot of lost opportunities but I can't remember the feel of your sheltering arms, what Kingdom of Stars! I can't dredge up the theories and tables of my education, but I'm mesmerized still by the line of your neck at the turn of the stairs, what City of Gold . . . !

THE FABLE OF EARTHLY ORIGIN

Your brain flowered, your eyes ignited, your chest thumped and I could see it fill and deflate in the incendiary air. Too hot to fuck. I stood before you hand over heart, naked beyond reckoning . . . You are my birthday suit, my salted caramel, we are the flag of my disposition, unfurled in morning light. Philosophy rests in the hollow of your hip, mathematics in the distance between us, burnt sugar, gyroscopic haunch, the fable of earthly origin, crotch sweat, rhythm dance, in the rush of the stream translucent crawfish, his mind, my mind, your indefatigable wish to walk as we do under spell of the forward-leaning arch, the press for a beginning, again, beginning again . . .

BLACK ROSES

A BENEFICENT LIGHT

I wanted to be a poet to rectify the wrongs exemplified by me. My giant cowlick, like a whisk of meringue, my misshapen shoes and necrotic toe, the lies I told to break a date with you, oh the black black heart of me. Fiends in the parlor, vampires in the kitchen. I wanted to be a poet to make my bladder sing, and soften my chambered guilt. I wanted to steal the glamour from my honeyed wig and stand on the platform in front of the desperate hordes, raising my hand to raise their faces into a beneficent light—sold by me. I can't repair and I can't forget the indignities so I catch a measure that resembles a form and cast a spell on my verses to stupefy the populace. Rain sizzles. Ergonomics hobble the diligent faithful. I cry lumps of tears to mobilize sympathy. I wanted to be a poet to validate my loss. I wanted to feel how generosity feels and know the satisfaction of melodious speech or melodious text, and feel the surprise of a couplet's close and bow my head to the patrol of grammar and the glorious missile of syntax. Forgive me for extending my metaphor and using description to bolster commentary and commentary to shore up the nouns. I'm penetrated by language and screwed by my natural rhythm, what's to be done? I'm here to represent the real with my ass in the air . . .

JANUARY

And if this is the wash of ages to clear the court—my leg dragged during the day, shook at night—then down the body, grow down, to feed the lower from the upper . . . I saw the incline and proposed a change of regime—adjutants of the sunrise, lost boys and weeping women—fields of black roses turn red in the slant of morning . . . I remember you before I met you, our feet in the escape position pointing in the same direction—my new shoes with their strips of suede, I fall anyway, look good in the diagonal air—the velocity at work under the roots of the elm . . . you catch your breath on a vision of mounting green waves tall as rockets, sweeping you up to the down with your gray eyes wild open, following the unanswered answers in the new rush of makeover time . . .

MY HOME THERE

What squeezes sound out of the swooping gulls?—ricochet rooftops—so that inside my head a wing tip slashes balance, I fall to the blue floor exhausted by my seventeenth attempt at flight. Who am I? A bastard son of the wind. Who am I? A capsule of time in a swipe of regret. Who am I? The margin of error and the tomb of pleasure and bottomless erasure. Who am I? I am Squirming Bird—hatched on the fifth eclipse to the sound of shrieking gulls—but some people call me Twiglet. *Hey Twiglet, your mother sucks birdseed. Hey Twiglet, there are skid marks on your face mask. Yo, Twiglet, your prick just ran off with a goldenrod.* I screech to a stop and inspect my claws, adjust my scope to the scorched ground: stunted oak trees sit like fireplugs in the dust of crumpled leaves. Who am I? The shadow of emptiness cast on a pink wall. My home there—infanticide nest—yes I did it—blood has dominion—where a jury yea or nay will deliver me out of this insufferable forest—*selva oscura*—out of this trapdoor, out of this shrink wrap, out of this sinkhole, this stink bomb, this tar pit, this colossal blunder, out of this wipeout, this piss pot, this interminable dirge . . .

A WORLD IN MOTION

Once I said I was a sailor as if my words were a world in motion on my back as I held the birds at bay who had tasted the blood of a lie. Birds will fly united in their lust to drink the blood of lies. A beak is a point of no return; I kept my face in shadows. Deep weather in a twisted feather—on the updrafts: scarlet talons . . . When you were my bird you swept the air clean of false judgments, contrary accounts; drank my blood in secret to protect me from the mob. Squawks and squeals in a thundercloud-cathedral afloat in the Alps of light. Your wing: my shield, your wing: my armor, your wing: my grace . . .

A JUNCTURE IN TIME

The wisdom of that dog in his flipped-out joy as he wiggles and licks where I sit on the stoop in my solitude shade as an arbor of fluffy afternoon light like his softest fur in the steady wash of traffic incoming outgoing as my life is outgoing in its delicate form as a body turning over as verses turn at the end of a line with a rhyme or a juncture in time or a stop for a breath in mind slow as the living unwinds where the frolicking pup is in my high though deep in the safety of somebody else's guard where he waits in the thrill of a wildly wagging tail for the cue, the sound, the gesture of hope in the jangle of keys or the lift of a body at rest standing up or a call of his beautiful name that is all his as he races and streaks to the opening door down the stairs in a tumbling dash to the steps of the stoop where I've stopped for a breath on my walk in the afternoon air . . .

THE END OF THE BEGINNING

Let's say you're a filigree on the pistons of radical love. I can smell your sweat from a block away, my nostrils flaring like wings of the dove. A rhyme is not inevitable but heat makes it stick. There's murder in the air and a toxic plume of itchy red regret. I can see it reflected in your nomadic eyes, with the corners of your mouth curled up like a garland or cast down like a sunken boat. It's mesmerizing—I love it—I hate it—What is it?—on a clear spring Thursday with wind topping the cottonwood trees and the crows arrayed in a phalanx of surrender. A rhyme is inevitable when your wig flies off in a gust like a runaway kite: it's a speck on a desperate flight in the towering light. I forget who I'm talking to in a suspended relay of attraction and retreat. But there you sit with your eyes pinned back to see the avengers rising from the floor. You're my ghost for all time, with your rictus set like a hockey mask and your heart sliced open to the core. In the vast structure of chance a rhyme is a return to paradise. I wipe my hands; I couldn't ask for more.

HER WORLD

The fire of one mind splits the world. She is leaning on the back of her bentwood chair refusing to sit; she will not be complicit by relaxing while the ashes drop. Too late, she is too late, the world has split beneath her hands—one world, ten worlds—which one is hers—accidental alien—the planet she came from is an empty rock spinning in space. She smooths back her long hair and tries to focus: *where do I dare to land, where are my friends now, what pale creatures and ravenous trees . . . ?* Too late she is too late, the future drips from her hands with each choice, *what has the one mind done, how did we fail*, she brushes past an iceberg in her living room, "I was honest," she thinks, "up to a point. I was attentive," she muses, "to a certain extent . . ." In the gap of her efforts, in the rift, in the ocean roaring, tide building, where she is slammed against the rocks and shattered, she remembers a spring day with plum trees blooming in pink clusters, and bodies splayed along the downtown streets stiffening in the sun. . . Nothing equals anything; her world is gone. She stands resolute, imperfect, undone. Leave her there, occupying empty space. There is no ending.

THAT

I wanted him to be that. Slowly I began to thaw. Stumbling through the darkness he remembered light. That person with that body. I had a data plan held over my head as if I too were a calculation. Who can believe who can be believed? He wanted to hammer him into submission, to free his past from poverty in a glittering vision of beating the odds. I wanted my own speculations, my own booms and busts. There was a split meeting, a conundrum of confidence and loss. They each went their separate way without looking back. Now they look back.

HERE

The distinguishing characteristics of the moment: light fog, fog-light—how you come to watch yourself, dangling from the first person, an actor of the utmost conviction disappearing tooth by tooth. Am I the dangler—confidence shredded—or is it you that I watch, fingering your suspenders and counting your diminishing toes? . . . I'm ready for all the changes—with my make-up kit fresh from the butcher and my cloak of invisibility rolled up like a cigar: watch me as we fade from view. You could say I was here emphatically, lived independently, loved precariously, loved maniacally, loved diversely, lived instinctively, loved decisively, lived multifariously. Then who is the shadowy person addressing the mirror? I watch your parts and pieces separate and drift to the ground like moths. No marker, no stone, no last words or first words, no haunting melody, no lingering sweetness, no dirges, no dances, no sign. Nobody remembers anything; they just make it up . . . I was here . . .

THE ESCAPE

Are we beginning again or is it all over, does the perpetual rain on you crimp your shots, your parries and thrusts, your fastballs and sliders, your nothing-but-the-nets? Yo is for you, and woe is for we. Oh is for us, B is for begin again . . . threw himself down on the sofa in a slash of sun—contemplating the cosmos, the human speck. Dear friend, dear population, what is the endgame, I lost the map of moons, how do we know when we arrive, who says we're here, where's here and who's that? Are we starting once more or is it finished, are we finished? I'm done with ornamental grammar, strip the sentence down to its noun and verb, a thug of meaning. On the solstice we ran to the beach to watch the ocean devour the sky; we escaped with no clothes and a taste of oblivion. Don't look up.

IN THE SKY OF THAT NAME

for Dawod

I. IF YOU WERE

If you were, as you were, in the sky of that name—*my* sky—as the Spring months unfold—If I were, as I was, in your sight, as the springing months fly, and your eyes—uplit by the sky of that name—so that everywhere—in me—I fly—If you were, as we were, if we were . . .

II. WHAT THEN

Not memory not fantasy not fact . . . what then . . . of that face . . . inclined to my light in the light—what then would rise out of bed—if there *were* a bed—inclined toward the window in the window's light—so that if a face turned away in shadows—to escape in the leftover dark?—Oh face come back to bed . . . what if nobody got up forever . . . if there *were* a bed, a face, the light, the window, in the leftover dark . . .

III. EXIT THE KINGS

By breakfast or dinner by coffee or tea asleep while awake . . . are you there? . . . If by the pillow in a stream of text—where is the shaping breath?—the hollow of the hand at rest? . . . am I there? . . . If by pulling back the drapes—what I thought I knew or made to see I think—you soak up light and work the shade . . . rolling in sheets of blue . . . as in a cave, a copse, a temple apse, a sanctuary hold, an ancient chambered mound cracked open underground . . . Exit the kings . . . as powder in a blast of sun. Done.

IV. THE MIRROR

Where was that was that you in my eye wait let me close my eyes yes it was you. Wait is that me in my eyes in the mirror yes I saw you there I held myself in high esteem as if you licked my eyeballs clean to reinvent the man I was . . . Wait that was me with my tongue out like a wagging pup to take you down to the bone and make you new to see myself in you . . . Wait that was you sucking me in like a noodle to fill you with my idea of you . . . if that was you in the sky where I was looking . . . Wait yes you are the sky and I am higher than blue in the mirror you had me make to see yourself higher than blue as you do . . . If that was you with your face and your eyes in my sky . . . in the light of the light of the mirror we made . . .

V. MADE OF MIND

Made of mind made of light made of raw skin in the blind world made of flickering words on a moving page on the tip of the tongue at the same time made of beds floating on borders of salt made of yowls on the pink desert bluffs for family and kin and the unbreakable bonds beginning to break made of suction way down below and the othering the othering—shot at the border of what mind to prevent what thought?—made of shoulder blades trying to fly in the sand and the grit and the grease of the flat world, made of gravity looping and your face in half-light waking in the dim world now getting lit made of sky-face and pure volition in the last world if we could if we were—made of flickering light awake in the half-lit world . . .

VI. NO END

As if parentheses—giant wings of time—or no time—or no fact—as if a song were sung to raise the body on air . . . my *there!* No map no geological features no roads, doors, a few implacable borders, and sky. If I say "face" which way do you turn? No end, no fractured faith . . . Two halves make two wholes . . . Hello . . .

VII. THE VANISHING POINT

That bird . . . in my sky . . . you opened—slice of a wing—to open your sky . . . If you could (if we were) run down the beach, seize the lifting breeze . . . Skies not yet opened . . . drift . . . in place . . . or so I've read—(books are wings)—the vanishing point calls to dreamers in the hierarchy of distances—the arcs we make, we made, such immaculate spheres, such small legends . . . tiny circles as you break into speed, bolt in the blue light you see . . . in the sky . . . wings are eyes . . .

VIII. THE GOLDEN HOUR

"Love is the golden hour" where we are *in* it in our same dream, that we have the same dream with us in it. I was awake I had to visit him in that land to sing a song in his ear as if gold were a sound . . . That we can cross the planes of sight that we can roam through realms and ride the night to find our bodies shaking and awake in sleep or if inside me, my dream of you, as if the late afternoon stopped at the apex where gold light spread I had to go to him in me and whisper in his ear of mine as if traversing worlds as if there were no walls "love is," I seemed to sing, as if your ear were here, "the golden hour," as if the hour were now, and you are dreaming me . . .

IX. BUT LET ME PULSING IN MOONLIGHT

But let me pulsing in moonlight awake to structures of musk—and the overblown vamping lamp curving to light up his face—oh from another dimension of music and color—with a dusting of midnight pollen—almost cut loose from where we were we are—unfolding anew in the sky of that name—this morning aloft, spreading-out power uprising . . . aurora air . . .

SELECTED POEMS

from THE NIGHT SUN

WOMAN ON FIRE

for Lily and Millie

I.

Lady * Queen * Doll * Woman

Using these words
not to belittle women
not to mock them.
Not to speak about women at all;

to speak of ourselves.
Unnamed regions—
    rose-pink and rust fire—
beyond the stern
and arrogant borders of manhood.

A shortage of terms, perhaps.
Language caught
in the vice of opposites, of only
two, so that what is not
man in us
we call *woman*.

II.

More than words. A time
when the Forbidden Tongue itself
is too vague.

All right girl—
                    what do you look like?

In the womb
an idea grows, fleshes itself
with fingers, eyes, toes,
useless at first;
dressed for future living.

From the darkness, magnetized,
of second-hand stores and hidden closets
facets of a new figure
gather.

Cherry-print red jersey blouse.
Ankle-length tight black skirt.
Black pumps, charcoal-grey hose,
pink crepe sash, black feather collar,
cherries in my ears, cherries
in my swept-up hair.
    Not the way I would have dressed.
    The way she came out.

And scuttled full blown
down the sidewalks of Castro St.
a queen like the ones she used to applaud.
Crooked her knees and
cried to the passing crowd
aaiy aaaiy thrilled
by the heat of her new body, too hot
for even herself to bear.

Out of the carcass of male dominion—
a revelry—
all across the City,
Halloween-risen from secret grounds,
fabulous women appear.
Immaculately conceived.
Spontaneously generated.
Out from my routine blue-jeaned drag
steps a 1930 Argentine Jewish Princess
— Inez Goldberg!

Tribal magic.

The next day, freedom
in my chest,
one great bird flown from my ribs,
a new soul born.

I laugh—of course! Adam
to my own Eve.

III.

The Chukchi people
of northeast Siberia
choose their shamans,
who are priest-magicians,
almost exclusively from homosexuals
who dress as women,
work as women,
and marry men.

Prophecies
from our profane mouths.
Rituals of dancing feet.
Refuse the limits of social inheritance
call upon women
to ignite their spirits
inside our willing bodies.

Iceland of Siberia, glistening tip
of the known world.
An igloo fortress
of frozen lace.
Glow from within—white heat
of prayer.
Woman on Fire.

IV.

Woman on Fire!   *Woman on Fire!*
Rob chants it   all night long,
dis/charges of energy, wild
under our sober men's clothing,
blood coals,   river
beneath the straight-jacket
of male skin.   *Woman*
on Fire!   Let down
your raging hair.   *Woman on Fire!*
Until this chanted
symbol is made real:

    rises into the room
a Latino queen
in red-feathered majorette hat
and pink-plumed body cape, adorned
with Christmas lights.
Who walks up to a wall socket
and plugs herself in—
Burning star-speckled
    everyone is awestruck
electric rose-bird!
    we are squealing in delight
Woman on Fire!
The Light!   The Living Light!

And there races back
and forth across the party
instant sympathy, a revolution
of untold ecstasies.   *Woman on Fire!*
until each one of us is
crowned
by her perfect queenliness,
Woman on Fire!   vision
of our own flaming selves.

MAY, 1975
SAN FRANCISCO

PILGRIMAGE

I was no earth
he travelled upon,
rested his head.

I did the walking.
my palms
asked questions

his flesh rose or fell
in response,
                        this way, here,
a shifting of land towards

the hills,   his nipples
unexpected rising,
all the gliding brown skin blown

from those charged points,   current
     straight to his heart.

Night over night my desire
imagines not the heave and grasp
of my own body, but his
form,   a geography,   where

I wandered,   hand-first.

ON THE WAY OUT

You tap on my car window, wave
a cheerful hello. Aren't you a little
late?
            I burned
everything you touched months
ago, letter by old letter dropped
sizzling into the toilet-bowl.
Baby, you were crispy
done away with.

      Now you wanna
talk my lips are sealed
with ashes, nothin to say.
Used to be
I could get hard just grazing your skin.

CINDERELLA

Last ditch
of hope, plain girls
aflame with wishes. The ballroom
is incandescent.
Straining for glory
each one, and only
one can.   only one.
                                        Against such odds
a woman buckles, she can no longer
hold the lie true to herself, runs screaming
a slipper of tears scattered behind.

The Prince must have more. Inquisition
storms the land.
Each must pit her pain
against this image of crystallized sorrow.
The oldest sister in desperation
cuts off her heel
but the shoe won't stay on
for all the blood.
The second sister cuts off a toe
but her heel's too big.
Cinderella, toying with madness
slips right in, fits
for the moment.
No more sweeping ashes?
She is taken away, the toe and heel

accepted as medals
for the herald's treasure box.

Her two sisters
lie mutilated in bed
sucking the blood-orange of the moon.
Cinderella
dances. Her satin gown
gets stiff from sweat
and itchy.
                How charming
is this man?
Where, she wonders
where are my sisters?

IN RUINS, INTACT

Based on scenes from the movie Hearts and Minds

I.

Raping a country—
            Literal words.
In a Saigon brothel a soldier
pulls at the nipples of his Vietnamese whore:
"This one has big knockers."
pulls at the triggers
of these two bombs, exploding fiery
into her flesh.   The metaphor
is too exact.
Even his face
is an anti-
personnel weapon.

II.

Who would have thought
such a perfect fountain
who would have   so much pressure
would have thought   two feet
into the air a column
of spurting blood   who
from a casual bullet to the brain
who would have thought   the heart
of just one man.

III.

So much time lived, so much
time left to cry over.
Two old women,   sisters.
One's home bombed away
the other's—spared.
One woman begins to weep
How will I live, how support myself.
Panic blossoms
        across her face.
Her sister stares ahead
expressionless.
One woman surveys the rubble
        —nothing stands
where everything used to be.
So much time lived, so little
left to cry over.
The other woman gazes,   no words.
Wipes a racing tremor
off her forehead.
What secrets known
to dodge the fateful falling
death from the sky?
    One life in ruins.
    One life intact.

In the midst
Of random fury,
                    only an outright
refusal to be destroyed.

THE TWENTY-NINTH BATHER

Dancing and laughing along the beach came the twenty-ninth bather,
the rest did not see her, but she saw them and loved them.
—WALT WHITMAN

When the white star in the distance
zoomed into view as a silver stallion, and the Prince
dismounted,   rosy and bold

and bent his hot lips
down to the virginal beauty, slabbed
                    at his feet
                                        I
                                felt the blows of
his breath on my mouth,   I stirred
into motion, rustled my skirts
and rose,   fluttering
ever after.

When the high-school girls cheered
the swimteam on to victory
I was with them
cheering.

When the high-school girls
talked about their boyfriends, I was with them
listening.

When the boys moved their dates
into the backyard
backed them up to a wall
      and sweated-out those
first kisses,   sweet menace
I was there
                    like a ghost with my girlfriend
watching
the boys.
And faithfully

each morning
real casual
I folded my clothes into a gym locker
and before dressing,   with studied
aimlessness   brushed—by knee, or arm, or back—
Joe Zalinsky's
neighborly pink cock.

They do not think
whom they souse with spray.

from GIVING UP THE GHOST

RAVING NO. 3

Would hold you all
    but my fingers are chipped
they don't reach.

Fingers pluck at me
    a Marilyn   the lust-demons have found.
sudden desperation: four walls
of fingers.
            Hunger comes
into a metaphor it
impels   A love-sandwich
from all sides
spinning.
        orbit
of entrance and exit.

But Mama they're fucking me where there are no holes!

RAVING NO. 9

There's a crowd of people / great / makes you feel lonelier.
You head into the wind of foreign voices
with 10 gallon hat & Disney ears, eagerly shaking hands
faces turn away, *"is he kidding?"*

You turn away from yourself, argh, a crowd
of selves   hatching, taking a look, & fleeing
the rooster who stands naked, wrinkled, in the middle.

A snake bites his tail,   the venom circuits.

O too little to do the too much work to be done!

RAVING ON, NO. 12

Beetle-browed:
                    eyebrows crawl
across his forehead stop
          at opposite ears
start buzzing

Words
crackle out of silk cocoons
     tunes of meaning
               strung together going nowhere

Rave on.
a corkscrew out of the mouth
in tongues, spiral
          drilling through skull.
What looks like a tunnel
is just one groove   going round
& round
               a wind
of syllables
bristling antennas in the inner ear

RAVING NO. 13, ALL HALLOWS' EVE

The ghosts come out of the walls like cockroaches
little winds pass you by waving
words, diaphanous, to see through.
The big eye winks
her sky lid:
                    Come with me kid.
          wail
of the woman next door fucking the
way *SHE* likes it.

Let those silk cats out of their paper cages!
We put on new
faces to frame an idea of love!
                    Tropical fish in the nightbowl
wandering iridescent   glamorous
done-up to be seen doing it.
                    Storks over the hillside stepping
village to village

dropping white feathers

          Beaking the moon

RAVING NO. 16

Dammit   you fit!
no ideal
construction I make
has the power to nestle in
like you do,   bird's nest,   cradle.
A fact
either proves a theory

or develops its own. My arms
want to shriek out:
          one grabbing
          the other stiffing: Stop!

our stomachs rub together.
those little hairs as I stroke
the planed wood of yr back.
A body
either proves what you have to say

or just goes ahead anyway.
my heart is in my heart.

RAVING NO. 25, VERNAL EQUINOX

The body lies down with the bicameral mind
in the split field of
    darkness & light.
half of each over blackland
half over white.
In the harlequin procession of stars
some shiny globe is traced by a shadowy partner.
We all reach the equator at the same time
have our heads in frost
    our distant feet in ice:
                                        Cut, tattooed, & hot-belted,
across the middle.
                                        The right brain-lobe
makes the left hand Shake.
O Shiva! Let all things equal their fearful
opposites! O Goddess, let earth
be where Heaven & Hell give up!

CRETAN BOY

There is no whole story.
She bends to tie her sandal.
He crooks his marble hip.
nothing more.

But the man who made
the boy, sucked in the world around him
breathed it out again,   condensed
by fingers, chisel, & stone.

He can't hide himself
in the planes & globes of the marble boy.
There IS a whole story
in the making
of the image—story of the maker.

Because one line goes too far.
Around the smooth-faced ass
between the cupped stone
under the flesh that hovers like planets
    over the tensed thighs
the line does not stop,
separating cheek from cheek.
                                                Deep
into the stone the sculptor's
fingers probed—into the tender space only

practiced fingers know.

plunging

into the loving image
up into the veined
marble *inside!*

from THE GRACES

MULTIPLE HEART

The figure of falling, falling forward, the figure kneeling, hands on dirty concrete, palms down, or the forehead touching grass. An agon of reconciliation: submission, the rapture of falling. Who captures you forewarned, a tongue's embrace, the wagon or welcome mat for real, to fill you with what you failed to realize, the God grants the God mercy to pardon the God.

regenerate is off the body's own sickness twist
among the *poudres* of tranquility the spasm
releases its beads, unsprung, the rosary
held tight revealed as rose garden

So the moment opens wide we call
present is blossom here & there in field   return
again & gain to process
dispersed

Before the acquisition we had to dismantle the wall, which did not fall (as she said) nevertheless was hung with monstrosities. And these we keep in corners under covers   my Baby was sitting by the refrigerator in white undershirt dazed after sex, glazed with lotion, swimming inside sea extended post-act like smell. He tried to hide in a quilt. I made him quit the quilt. His wall was overhung, I said Baby come into the light where my actual love is shining   then I saw that what he was lovely effortless in hairdo accidental slant of strands impeccable fall

Not to be beholden to anticipation
either in length or breadth, breath of ashes
equal to any infusion of sustenance,
the spore regales the fungus with tales of air
Certainly there is any sure way, in loping movement
as flash, & the ineptitude of synapse or
inevitable flow of old silence calls forward
as it will, the will to forward

that, as it should be, determines exact
juncture, fall of foot, root, wing, or bone
Some are many & some alone or none to
call the heart a heart, spade a spade, jeweled
with precision each, when get to it, fruitless seed
you thought was broken blossoming out of dead wood

and love shall love shall love shall over all incumbency dominion, idle caresses rose-lipped & minds locked fierce eyes piercing. I have had all & it shall, has taken me anew   recumbence in fire, licked salt, bushes, bruised, swollen tips, the drift my flesh takes is thought's deepest desiring   sighs well up as intellection springs. Love shall be called forward called all, being now inside hegemony among each blushing word the truest touch of tongue's frail blessing restricted in no sense wise or not, tears running down face at mere mention of her name, his glory, (my Hera)—this was, as was, long ago, I was reading, she had chunky solid cracked the clunky case, refracted speech, and so she had she did. It made her great. & only one among the ones before who stand before in largeness, bulk, extravagant vastness we meekly seek to emulate in song. How stabbed he was, for me, because my master called me slave. How thoroughly, I said, deliciously, I slave to master.

O that river song green came through again body bountiful, that lay back in the arms of water I also called breast, beautiful to merely look, mere looking raised to real sight, floating without acceleration or goal, baking little cookie of self in shell evaporating—tender thing. Inside the book the river runs into itself again again. I took my own self to the headlands, crawled along the dusty ground, ground my bare back into the dust.   Who was there?   He was. With me.   We swam away together. O that river, flung in ribbons, ran, runs, will run, the rungs of pleasure ascend the midday as if water flowing upwards flew

# # #

bereave me, you fall, that like me down to nothing
ground or grovel, where
can such as we gain sight & rise to triumph operatic
bird's call, fawn's poise, quail's quackle, & such as nature's
    nonrational folk
(radishes too) do, & find themselves in peace, or work, without
    intention,
with grace of necessity.   I have this.   I don't intend, I must.

Ah we, let down that rope of words & I will climb . . . !

I remain unconvinced by anything that hangs, so especially that kind of hover over the tall trees, when didn't want to reach the cabin before she ate his finger, like a bone as it was, poor skinny kid. Reduce to beleaguer the craft of lying, as if no intention mattered as matter, or moment of conviction that everything he said covered something else, all the way from then. He was judiciously upset, as trust is really the matter of love to stay, that shouldered head. Bring me to the lip that lisps, I'll cover for it.

phrase making in musical sequence made ready the declamation
of souls, beside the racked body—wreck of passage—who done
together themselves as the other, or other as other, in stance against
open-purpose ride. they took moral, made it normal,
& we left
(that vocabulary

quite a difference between the freedom you feel and the freedom
they allowed you, they gave you for DEAD, their flower, over grave.
This time was different—the clifftop & reef, wind blowing peli-
cans eye-level, in consequence of sight unPLANNED. Man, this
boy is quite a woman. See time, and that with aquatic   ballet
seconds . . .

Too close for comfort yet comfort calls, pulls closer, knit, hug, perfection. She however old, and he, however old, or both both, meet, entwine, form-ally relate. Driven of hunger, shitty work conditions, shame of race, or size, or vocabulary, close over mouths as bedquilt soften, that stretch and grade of touching. He takes her into his arms where she in his arms has her arms full

# # #

1) remainder indifferent to uplift eyes
or gold leaves by goddess still fall
Under the gaze of Watcher. Thematic uprisings,
underscore   three images on a black bough.
blecch. Entire opus corpus deliciously vague, feel.

2) recovery mandated by urgency of the woof
hand fed, pedaled, pale egg-yellow that cries for pink.
Cries, alas (*hélas*!) cries hard. White fire
laps at edges of page, curling embittered lips.

Where was going is not become
as each every direction justice demands its own attention
bleeding pen, wiped on sleeve, chin up, ahead
filled with the meaning of its momentum, slug of sound
Gulp. Gulp that draught of wind to dwell in ear
In balance with pulse, spurt, synaptic process, gorge
What—nothing to do with anything so organic as *mind*?

Lily of lights fell down to rain slice
the rear ear reared in delight, skidded.
End up to the bumper—any pretty image—queens in
working-class apparel, actual blood lines: pricked skin.
My mother is dead. *Meine mutter ist tod. Adio, io moro.*
This is true, will be true, insistence tells
insistence. Follow the fellow who follows the fall.

radiant organicisms meant implications of meaning, vertebrate conclusions, as this side mirror'd that with only a slight jokey curled lip, raised brow. So that's how measure falls beneath the wheels of chance, some big ol' loco-motive-ation, raw slumbering doom. I love your eyes, your face and feet, though why I can't describe the smell implicit in your lazy airs, illicit turpitude and silence ringing my jaw, ache of tooth, spring of bone. the only matter is at hand.

Foregone and in conclusion the most, that drippy feeling in the center of the hand (black dot), because and such connectives are, I leap upon you on the bed right now, pull up the page. Darling is gross, and darling is tall, and all intimations of mortality centered between your teeny breast which do not blink but stare relentless immortal throughout the flesh and land of senses slaver, silver luscious core. How am I lost and how adore the music of your sphere.

# # #

a rod around, the cough implicit in the cloth of solitude, broad enough and bent to that desuetude of sighs, the underpants shucked. A leafy vessel and a marginal rose, a platitude on which the whole delight of loving rests (chopped head), and so comes forward, and so it does, the rude awakening of a blank face crowned with doe eyes, the utter amazement of mask in tension with what it hides ("the terror of earrings"). Reclaim the solitary window from which a face peers watching snow, appears outside in drifts falls down and traces wings of an angel in shades of white, licking the lips, and rubbing the shoulder, and kissing down there where no one knows . . .

O light-faced scintillating marjoram, sweet breather and above all blest, to sneeze in the face & fly, run naked playing children's games of chance. So that and how it was, along lines of sight only possibly described as endearing, a head cradled in arms, a head on a breast, & all the surreptitious delicious dialogue of eyelashes. For that, & because of it, the nausea of unstoppable giving, the rectitude of the blood organ's unflapping lift. Seize all papers & shuffle to feel wind, relax as I said the *explication de texte*. Marvel the agile dream of a life filled with consummate confrontations,   next words . . .

I came down from the mountain hanging by anything that remains, for the crucial step in deliverance is a loose neck. I've emptied myself of the sign (valentine) & am now living stupidly without the ache of history. & that's how it should be! cries the impending sentence: Me Me Me Me   forthwith   and for all that, the blossoming emotion of a blood-swelled phrase. Hard on the heels of love comes rushing a new word . . . crux   anima   vacate soporific   flux   boon

ramada, ramada, let down your golden hinde . . .
as in the beginning what saw was, when saw, a fabulosity
in temperate drag. (the desire to be used by language to the fullest
extent it knows how)   Ho jo to ho! the lost sounds fill with meaning
in the flatulent air

rarity   that remains in light   that swishes and flails

and remains in light

the morphology of greed, or some such hunger that clenches the fist, transmogrifies the brow. towards the ocean and all faces blended in sorrow, or uplifted to that purple sky, the same sea. who was there, not me, and who was there, was me. the foreshortened delight of a face face to face with a face, came rushing through the temperate zone alone together with fingers splayed. How the light changes hour by hour, eye by eye, when contact keeps the form intact, and when light falls out of the clouds from stuttering belief one face in the light framed by halo's skillful detention, the pure pleasure of wishing it so : open

# # #

When the existence repeated in same phrases came apart at the
    hinges,
reconstituted in helical bonds that spiral known as the bigger
    bang, fresh
        discover each turn
        returns axis central
        glance off light, the
        shining, seen anew each particular
sentience, flavor, ridiculous in extremities, compact in allegiance, in
favorite bondage (the dispelling of logic in favor of magic), old
    monstrosities
come apart in the hands to reveal the workings of inner beauty,
    stupefying
exactness of the loop-de-loop courting the air . . .

I remember the paintings from their places on the wall, voice of
a secretude.
and then the fable about a boy and all his lack of hair, some
idiotic
punchline at the conclusion of a punch. Heavens that heavenate
above,
a comparison between one good thing and another, the trickle-
down effect
of a bright eye over high cheekbones—then give me that thing.

Whenever that corruption comes to take me in the arms of its
vicissitudes
I roll in my worminess down the hole as the world turns, so wounds
the slothy membranes, all of a suddenness my corruptions fail me.
Let in the purity
of the loving heart's stupidity: all is good, needy & beauty

The exceptional liftoff of a rocket rammed with a personal hand, a little language of sighs. or a fever that starts with an itchy palm leaves off mid-phrase in a decapitation of the text. The best becomes better only with care, implicit in the infolding of tongues, and the one who goes knowingly down to desire is the one who knows better in the end. Then I look at you as your tongue is lolling, as my own tongue sticks to its gum. For every little leaf that inches a bud, formidable in the face of winds, I notch one notch in my tightened waist, say "now I am beautiful" not because you make me, but because I see you so

This delectable shortage of terminal junctures, something like a rose of Castile working itself into full bloom. and after the hip, the saving of face in a pressed album all eyes read as a turned table revolving its disc, some eerie melody connoted by an ascending riff. then the borrowed conjunction of a narrative and its moving parts, a skinny fellow all elbows swimming in a salt sea. or a science of phraseology measuring separate parts of the tongue, where every descent is a nascent plot: the coming to grips of a fanned lady in a crowd of samurai, or some lonely bugger casting his leaves to the wind. this where we were or are a fine glass for scrying, relating the crossed beams of starry eyes, or a story of eyes crossed, flush with the influx of sentences lacking periods, turning and burning in the swirl of a fire that holiness must seek heaven . . .

One step releases the world. The fire of magic in her eyes lit up the external valves. Invisible to all but the naked eye the naked world trembled in its shell, I beheld the Well of Seeing with a steady gaze. And Rebecca that sang on the desert lip, whose luster of voice eased the parched jug, who wet the men and made them squirm, that stood ablaze in the heat yet cooled by the blue in the black of her hair. Became now before us where we assembled a figure of speech to haunt our desolate ears, in which dim lands immaculate violets grow, colonizing that mulch and loam with a swagger loaded into the rifts of purple ore, a purple of such redness as even her lips may envy . . .

from A'S DREAM

CITY OF MEN

I heard my name, the day rose and disappear over the beach. the day on each breath tasted my food, that night roll slowly cover in the cool, his face around my breast. the day inhaling grow pale and disappear, water on his way, up the shores hissing. under the night stillness inclined my morning beach, undressing my friend of liquid, my most same. at evening while whispering from the bed by me, his way was accomplished. his full perfect arm a health of ripe waters. the day received moon laughing, love lay me that night.

love growth, manly types have been young men, my year my nights, comrades. projecting tongues clear my world; I feed, tell all the secret, offering delicious profit away from the clank. respond myself for all the need secluded, from standards to pleasures rejoices. escaped here; paths clear to speak: I can spot men and exhibit as I dare fair warning. further affections perhaps destructive. expect your long room in the open air. on your kiss permit be carried into sleep, caught me that I have written this, go your hand on your way upon my hip, that hit I hinted at, perhaps more trial. put your lips back, new husband, who would sign himself a candidate for my affections? in hand one thing will be all, suspicious, destructive, give up all else, exhausting your conformity, troubling your hand from my shoulders. I gawk unborn with you on a hill; upon mine, lips, I permit your throbs; beneath your clothing I have escaped from me. which way? many times reading it not understand. some trial for I emerge uncertain, theory around would have to be abandoned. feel me go forth. touching is wood, is rock, is air sea island roof enough diligently sought it many year at random, among animals, lapping apples and lemons, pairing fitful grossest nature and what goes with them. yearning for any and attracting whoever you are. swimmer naked in the bath from head to foot and what it arouses, trembling curve and the clinch of hips, the mouth makes me fainting from exultation and relief, embrace in the night the cling of any man drunk eyes, the storm that loves me, by the pliant loins a moment emerging stars. blending each body from the gnaw, wet overture anticipating the perfect face, for myself from you two hawks in the air, waves of nearness, floating the divine list to possess a lawless sea. I yield to the vessel, sliding fingers and thrusting hands, warp and woof, victory and relief, close pressure makes excess divine. pushes anticipating the strain exhaust each other; side by side on the coverlet lying and floating. from that, myself, without which . . .

I have lived orgies and will one day make pageants. bright windows with continual feast: those eyes‘ swift flash as I pass. O I make rows of you, streets of you, processions, spectacles . . .

Boys up and down the road, priests of ourselves, wrenching and owning the other. fingers stretching elbows, alarming the air, making no law less than loving, ease on down fearless power the arm, the arm, sleepless . . . underneath what you say my measureless name . . . walks within him at night wandering with other men . . . ocean of hand in hand . . . tenderest pictures hang in my woods . . . another curved shoulder . . .

acrid river drain itself, blowing suppleness and strength from judges. milk commands mystery, moisture of the right man delights the earth, shame knows how to shoot for own sake. nothing lacking in gushing showers, warm-blooded rivers wrestle suns. deposit within me the pent-up winds of myself, crops from the birth of deliciousness, plant of you to awake at the touch of a man. greater heroes sleep in sex, wrap a thousand years in slow rude muscle of themselves, accumulated purities deposit gods on earth. onward pour the stuff; distill from the fruit of the fruit meaning's delicacies . . .

growing up above the tomb there, pink-tinged heart ascend the atmosphere; rise with it breast in your sweet way. behind the mask of materials take control of all, emerge under you roots of sound and odor, scented show folded in shifting forms. spring unbare this serve me lovers, conveyed essential shape inhale the bloom. burn and sting will not be freeze, reverberations give tone to delicate blood. exhilarating immortal death, inseparably grow and dissipate, last beyond all in comrade's body sighs in night in rage not subtle, dismiss chattering words to savage wrists. willful broken oath, nourishment of beating and pounding, defiances thrown in the wilds of hungry pantings. dissatisfied dreams of every day show dead words, limbs and senses thrown from heaving skies. not savage but cries and laughter, pulse of systole/diastole sounded in air a certain number standing alone, me twined around. it hung down and glistens there, unbending. wide flat companion of lusty oak makes me a little moss, stood for my sight and I grew wonder. lover in the dark brought to live green produce boys! greed eats me, wholesome bunch saturate my palms. mounting my friend, waist hanging over my shoulder, dripping spiral, the hot hand that flushes. encircling red animal, purple lurking thumb, paternity of liquid will be torment and tide. odor of lips glued together; curves, brothers, that feelers may be trembling sweats; visions lie willing and naked under the ripening sun. whitened with the souse of primitive men, sleep together with crushed mint and sap, climbers after body blow husks from indecent eyes, find themselves breasts and bellies up and down the night. hairy murmurs and firm legs match the man to mountain, climbing my man I light the hillside. toss him, plucked from chastity, to saturate the sea; all men carry men, lurking. tight pause and edge to pressure, roaming hand-whirl, I glow spontaneous, know what he is dreaming. the same content, airs intimate that fill my place with him, smell of wild relief, welcome falling . . .

two simple men modeled under full sail, splendor of one neck envelops the other. spread around me, crowd of glory, I saw the pass and kissed him appearances, after all, may be only speculations; identities are of the real. hold me by the hand, that is subtle air, impalpable, curiously words hold untellable. reason confound us, sense surround us, he travels to me and these are the shining things I perceive. I walk in the fable of a man, charged with points of view, skies of colors, densities, and something yet to be known . . .

Full of you and become you. any number could be me. read these and become a comrade. with you I am one

A'S DREAM

Here's where I came in, captive and their speeches. Anxious like any new moon, days away will be filled with dreams. From the main image its mood passing through its phases, a different mind immediately disrupted. Two will run between love and law. Her eyes must learn to see another's eyes. In the thrill of the wind shadows turn the pillars into trees. Flee the swirling house, free the following night. It rains on you, shaken to the horizon line.

*****

Beams can mislead as well as lead, spell out transforming mind. Great poignance shed tears of their own audience. Some floral names seem as if they're part of another dimension. Sensing an opening the cattle are feeding off drowned roses; what kind of boy is a changeling? He uses personification just as people do. With X lurking in the unseen air how safe would you feel? Approaching voices are heard. He's interested in finding them, not in dealing with them.

*****

The way things should be change places with sentimental remorse. Likes to sleep there, and that gives us the world upside down. Does you want to sleep there yourself, surrounded by the great economy of language? Scent around its delicate head seems good enough to eat. And now, having scoured the forest, will be losing more than this particular way. On whom go in and out revolving doors are hot on heels, the most flowery sweetness is ashamed of reason. From now on, tongue in the mud is a lover screaming for a serpent, or a window open to theatrical moonlight, or power-ground to pass the time, or a little nature tune about birds.

*****

Suddenly we know swoony music fools us. Her eyes entwined around the command of seduction attend his needs while his mortal body opens. Honey-bags explode their calm rehearsal, as the point, so ripe with perfect timing, flies away like fate. Learn from your own misgivings what you can learn from the mistakes. Tricks about the natural world pile up accusations, he feels murdered by extravagant phrases of information. While he sleeps a million fail, swollen by the evening star.

* * * * *

A twinkle never chooses the simple route. To his feet the goddess spouts cherry lips, white hand. In this changeable dark manipulations reveal the building-up of person; magic, of course, is astonished. As you laugh notice the entire surroundings resound with your barking. Ghosts in their proper haunts turn the ocean gold. Entrances and exits keep track of real questions. He sees something: this spot at once recognizes what they might be doing here.

MATERIAL'S DAUGHTER

I wandered away from my early childhood, framed by her massive hair. Officials rob and flog them; martyrs my guiding stars. I had had nothing, had had had nothing to eat; a comrade assured me he wasn't hungry. His intensity walked up the stairs, but beautiful things are necessities. Given work I marveled about the ecstasy music could create in me; I talked on, lanky daily struggle, customers of the grocery in discussions with an agitator and a nurse. Radiant voice contracted the first time into weeks of disclosure, anticipation and escape. Living things began to cry. I picked him up cooing. Think back; if you spill a drop nights pay the price. The operation did not take place.

But there was no other yard, fields, hills, purgatory. Cleaning gruff boots, scrubbing burnt almonds, so violently the room in a heap was put to bed and petted. Our lives were busy in foreign languages, beg from me public stories about scandal, toilers articulate a mysterious young woman on a truck. Led away whispered "the island of splendid bearing," flowers bumped into trees on the natural sidewalks. I read, I flung my arm, I too would go, I went in search, it was flaming, I hung on his lips, I was the speaker. Some pawnshop would find that evening revealed on the vanishing step, waving and snatched away from a very clear idea of material's daughter.

Economic categories picked up an entirely new type; perhaps on Monday a perfunctory letter shook an old woman free. Public opinion sat dumbfounded on many faces. He had immediately opened into unconsciousness but would answer no questions, a cry trying to open his mouth nearly broke the bullet. I found an article, the avenger, began pouring to beat back his thrusts, purity should hear and carried on a ferocious campaign to action. If only they knew she was being made to suffer for me. I knocked and informed me for a long time, startled by my looks. Nature could not extract that swelling in the throat. I gave an assumed name but wouldn't deny my identity – no no no, the yellowed paper was a strong young tree, I gulped coal and raised the hall to ferment.

In the afternoon I was told to wait; time settled into a small room; little objects passed into my mouth, childhood, schooldays, teacher, tender. Out of the window nothing had been broken—just flattened a bit. Human things reached motives in her estimation. I chose to walk, so many crimes fascinated me.

ELSEWHERE

I.

Listen!—the earth and roar, every mile off in the distance. Then with a piece of fat from a little bag he made a looking glass; with great care he contemplated the effect. "I shall kill it."

Children of the Keeper, of the Leader, of the One-eyed, the Terrible, the way is before us, no trickery! The light in you and eat shall argue, it was made—and he pointed to the north. Galloping clouds to a farther mountain, fired the mist, and followed him into the lightning.

"This noise is king! This noise is king!" thundered through the worship, the elders clapped their hands and ran away. The country grew in wreaths, diaphanous, burning vegetation, the sun odorous. Into square blocks are dome-shaped and built; men can walk six feet wide, surrounded at a distance by a circle of smaller stars.

It is good, we are weary, let us rest. Stepping into the milk, skinned and jointed. Turn and turn about, three of us flung ourselves, the sweet weary, and slept down.

As we were overtaken a horseshoe-shaped sunset, a smooth river ends there. No twilight, and the shadows shoot arrows. Mine has been a life, and we shall fall by the way. A hut is ready outside the town, "Unlimited," in a great grass city. Each of us was ready when we woke it. The spectacle standing behind us.

Stood still in the silence, in his right hand enormous silence. A girl came, bearing a red jar, boiling with "our lives depend on it." Still stood for a minute, projected an inch, and began to speak: "Listen, stars and storm and unborn words!" Hearts died away in a faint wail, including our own. "I smell it, I'm old on the ground, footsteps, footsteps—," she pointed to the mountains—"Not here, not stones, not gleam, strip off the features—" and was carried back into the hut

The great space, instantly ourselves, was empty. Windowless indeed, with the outer air driven through the roof. Running down the length of the place as my legs would carry me, I am free to own another five minutes. Enter it again, but he held me tight, I could not, stopped, became focused. "What is that thing? And what are those things?" pointing to the white company.

Very slowly one began to shake in the whole world. When our eyes grew used to it we followed.

II.

As far as the eye down the vapory horizon, line, square, triangle of lurid gold. Measureless cranes against a flying sky. And then the air quivered, turned round, turned over, and got him by the throat. The end fell forward and rolled for a minute. Afterwards, we managed ablutions.

I suppose I slept, yellowish and frizzed up; an old man hung loosely, eyes of paper and a look of monotonous snow. "Stranger" he said, "and by the way they teach their children foot language here. Come up out of the sea." I reached the motion of a drained lake. I saw no signs destined to be gratified.

We discovered the mouth was the contents, hollowed out by a steaming hand. We squatted, the skins ate with satisfaction, orders for destruction were set before us. "Pardon me" I interrupted, "How long is the fifth day of absence?" Watching for our appearance, they saw us come out smoking. Hung upon the wall all shapes were clarified. From a stem was passed the wood of constant attention, burning low. A palm tree showed silence contemplating the shadows.

He rose. There was no air, no furniture, running stone length. Get away, please hold me, I can't. This never happened, as we stood there literally. The other woman took a walk, shaped like a big spear. As time went on we descended from these men.

They had come forth in a giant cloak, muffled voices. Those who waited could tell no tales, but had power over all things. The land was "Households," resembling this stretch of swamp country.

I have been inclined once or twice on the time left. Something happened when I shut my eyes: chosen, beautiful, strong arm, happy face. Ask me what I saw. I love to wash your feet with bitter memories.

III.

They fell upon the white wrappings, hand on the rock. Night by night, soft or stiff, tossing in the slab-form of solemn sleep. Give strength to wander across blotted identity, burst in the past and melt echoing up the cliffs. He stood staring; partial stupefaction. "Cover it up and take me away."

Going to the shelf she bent down and loosed the man, her mouth tied up with a bladder kissed the head and chest. Fumes prevented us from seeing. The hour burst noiselessly, witness.

After some months, boyhood hardened, better than the old one. No ordinary marriage could give such wonderful shame and grief. In the face we had impotence, in the heart insolence; experience is possible. Leaving our hands down, we awaited earthly habitation.

Some spare boots, a rifle each, the appointed minutes. "We are ready," I answered, "though for my part I have no memory." A man in a nightshirt pointed out of the cave to a central path. Light did not consume our bodies.

A sheet of water appeared to descend, a mountain wall, and evident ruins. Remote a little more, we reached high through the sinking ground, filed across. Some idea of sight met our view, shrines and palaces and party walls. We came to a pile of fading light. I think I may as well have been a tangled thing, pressed enormous enclosing another of small size. There used to be a spot here; it has passed. While we were eating the moon—cold meat—thickness began to flood the place—I brought you, I can see it, I shuddered.

I brought you your eating; when done we will go out. The brooding days ran from our whispers, imperfections in all their majesty! Upon each other we poured forth the tale, a little untamed solitude.

There remains a basin in the outer court, ready to start. This man bowed humbly till we grew old. "Well, let him come, he will bear this." I slung a spare skin on my back till he had vanished. Quaking, we sprang from ledge to ledge. Angles gave the appearance of blown bodily movement. There was a humming sound beneath us, like a living thing. On our stomachs, grain of the rock, against the wind, we saw the other side. "That's it!" I groaned, crept, a wilderness of gathering fear. Clasping, I met my own and hauled.

IV.

The white day streamed across the plain. Heavy with blood, we rose and ate inward. Years stamped out the murmuring land, sting passed, story passes with it. I shall forget them; I forget them and you. Across the sea—another overshadowed path—a gathering song:

When he was thrown in with men: their history.
An attempt has been made, Chief of Incidents.
Something ignited the grass, up to their heads weeping.
His name does not matter.

His name does not matter: he went to bed.
We swept our heads through the curtain, a cutting wind.
Quick, this space wheels, they can never bear this cold.
In the shelter they vanished; you told them nothing.

You told them their spoor was obliterated.
What is to be done?
Look at this hand – it dropped slowly to the earth.
Quiver in their sound, but where are they now?

We saw a woman walking towards us, walked like a woman.
"How is your name and what are your people?"
"My name is 'fall by the way,' but I ran faster."
"My name is 'stood still and watched'," and he came forward.

Now I will tell you something more.
Now I will tell you lost in the clouds.
When we have stamped the earth flat I have spoken.
Grow fat in my shadow, the liar has spoken!

ALL THAT

He awoke with a pillow between sex and memory. He sat there, explained neither by substance nor dialectic. He found the red glow, touched a knob: in that second he was middle-aged. Hands outstretched, he began to retrace his steps.

Spirit should walk into that bedroom. In the beginning huge purposes had drawn him into romance, rub his temples through his reason, his tiny red beard. Trees—the young branch-like women and their ears—organs. His small eyes split in two.

He bowed his head with his hands, cafeterias, coffee. The details in which he dwelt subscribed to brochures. His father had come true in the usual way. He forgot why he could hear his own breathing.

The door opened: a bundle of clothes. He snorted, put on his pants, walked to the mirror. A former philosophic system prepared to take charge. We live forever.

SATURATED

Up the ravine the sun was choking with dust. Emotion on the windows from the sideways heat, breathless their heads hang—they've stooped—and went in through the low doorway. On this dark corner table two glasses. His bold cheeks, his full lips—the ox. He was looking beneath the sunlight; every object was almost cool in the stream. Into his hands his pockets threw their coins.

I found a few words about each; nickname, unmarried, career, places in a mist of obscurity. In our part of the country, no one knew anyone, visited anyone, had money, noticed much. There were puzzling forces, inactive, having iron control. I have met no one else.

He played with his moods like a toy, climbed out of his skin. His gaze softened his lips into flourishes. He grew embarrassed and burst into laughter. All their eyes uncovered his face; far away began to fly into the room.

Like a trembling finger, the path lay across the field. At low tide I saw long wings oblivious of us. Everyone opened, as if silence was his . . .

Talking loudly, splutter up in the air and wave—they kept on repeating, "Come on, come on!"; his face was transfigured across the counter, summoned over to happiness.

I went out; the film of heat hung black over the blue sky. The grass had left behind no wind, against the windowpane wet hair was dancing. New faces had collected in the room. The sky was walking.

from INTO DISTANCES

INTO DISTANCES

I.

The sky: the sea with wings. There have been days I would stand gazing for hours in diversity. From these fragments, from causes, power, poverty, I belong to experience.

She labored down the path barefoot, the wind wrapped her body, shadowed by clustering blossoms and velvety sunshine. I remember her unhappy married life as more children arrived, taking hold of me on all sides in one spot of my will—"stomp me into the ground." I lied, she was never close to the wind. The fat flowers laughed. I was hardened and have no meaning.

We looked: sweeping down the approaching road it grew louder, rushed against the flat earth roaring. Smell and hear and see and feel everything! I listened to the voice and knew it sucked up all the air around us. Slowly I was learning shame and secrecy, forced joy behind the henhouse, slept off something wrong, shook me nameless and struck my body with perfection and disgust. His word was enough for me, though I knew he'd never be his word.

My grandmother when there is no moon. She possessed all and assumed control, milked the cows with the movements of a man, skimmed under her hands the dawn and carried pistons to bed at night. In private no man could look her in the eye; her thick hair would appear in the door: she walked immune. At my tears she would use it on me: "You're unornamented girl!" That was long ago; I walk hand in hand with unloveliness that gave distinction to destruction. Anyone elaborated the story through my silence.

While the cold sky came driving down to the grass with dew, the men cut firewood, the women peeled and sliced. If you looked at them you felt as if you'd worked yourself, who pass greeting over the hills, family honor under the cedar trees, torture their wives, show no resentment, work again, hard filled with labor our house smooth as night.

Now around through the crowd on the platform music. His silver buckle distinguished him, he knew all the songs, he was young and called for the dance. Everyone bowed, separated, flaming light in the center they met, flying around and drifting clouds. His side, her face, her hands, his bending shoulder. I climbed before me a sea of swinging figures, rushed me under the raised legs and skirts. And the calling! . . . all the good things . . . listening . . . I was so little!

The slaughtering smoking winter filled mounds. You threw in a handful of corn and you could eat into deep plates. Was my name Standing Farther, Cooler and Tougher, Virgin Whiteness, Bleeding Arrows? Was there a secret tale in my voice that continued at midnight when the stars were creeping, quarreling into my child life money terror, dog work, disobey, placed my hand where we were not; tears fell on it.

We went by covered wagon, reached a forest, and stopped. Under the sky I stood on the yielding earth, her eyes were black, transitoriness came and swept the hills into distances. She stood facing north and west and south. I must turn around again and carry down words. It has been years with ease and swiftness. They came soundlessly over the wheel of the sky.

If you want to run away don't tell stories. She turned swiftly and gazed at her standing there. She could not hide the eyes still young and flared open. I began to make up a story—that eventuality between me and the door—pushed by the sky and some wind carrying me on its back. I would say I was walking down the road and slipped into smooth clouds, long time. We all stood and melted together, there where that black speck was gone . . .

II.

The town was occupied—Strike!—bullets flying on our side of the river. The law restored the convicted back in the ground. In the dark tunnels long hours dug and dragged it to the end of the month. I passed in a foreign tongue, ceaselessly preparing for another construction.

She kept her eyes on the edge of an excavation. I have seen that look in other eyes, in love with a terrible thing and submerged in another: I can show each night. The men mixed with clay—foul-mouthed and trusting—spent it in one night. She befriended the men, alone in the darkness humble before infinity. The lean one was one of these; the men exchanged glances; big to her and gleamed with smothered laughter. He called to me and I slipped in. We passed through a canyon, and you can have this horse I'm riding.

If you open a book you have to write in it. I fled beyond the bitter tracks we had made. The gleaming road leapt forward like water, moonlight ice with prairie grass and purple hills. Animals cried there, and stretched on stones. Beyond them mountains called the snows into crevices.

You passed empty houses—The Flats—coyotes left their hiding places. The saloon, the school house, the Company. Miners—boys!—eating and breeding; the next strike; hunger would not give credit. I heard the possessors deserve the world of knowledge. There was silence about her for miles, I remade her silence. She would turn without a word, would gather the hills, would follow the same tune unrolling in the wind. Once, I myself knew it, in one spot on the hard, packed earth.

She worked and buried her head at night, knew little of theory but turned loose her convictions upon them. Could she tear the petrified trees from the earth by their roots? It beat rhythmically, climbed the flight of stairs, the end of "education" and enemy of women, began to draw the veil of forgetfulness down over desire. I was my wind as I sit here with leaves about me. I wrote down my name in actions not suitable for position.

If they told a story I understood their purpose. Grave things drawn beyond their depths. As I wrote I recalled—a laborer can turn her hand—pushed upward, staring at it, connected, convicted. Words are nothing but words—then gradually they were streets. I walked, there were trees flowing, earth against my body, face down in work and sleep. And those up there: his mouth and eyes, my mother with mud, the company store. She had come before me, a woman and a stranger, muscular arms and wilderness under the skin. The word subjects her to the circle to be pure and repeated. Words cannot erase experience.

The train was an entreaty, but did not buy a ticket to leave. I marched and searched their faces. The lines—their falling music—would not be ended . . .

III.

At night the wind from the mesa could reach and I rode safely. Mingling with wailing to demonstrate "learned something." Yes, they are a part of her blood, forming far from town the cold lightning across my doorway. I erased those dead songs from my tongue.

Springtime, up the fuzzy hills, the river higher, rushing each night in our ears. In the semi-darkness the shouting between us was already filled. I cried out, waded under, crept nearer, clung to mine. Lights were burning like an animal that has eaten. The swaying water sailing away, hung in the willow trees, sated; in the morning the world is gone. Today is shivering, those were my blood and bodies, far back from the dark mountains in the flood.

Listen and look intelligent—you have grammar and a few more things, cook their food, wash bed, made skirts in her big-veined hands—a short distance from the rock rim for hours. Names and addresses contained patterns; from this shortlist I chose these working shoulders.

Ah!—house!—drive me over the hills tomorrow! One day my mother was sick and I must go home. Up the canyon road the scrub oak pulling at the frozen ground—only thinking, feeling nothing—separate units exhausted distances, down the lashing road must be coaxed a faltering child. I stumbled the steps, beyond the windows shattered into bits . . . three days and nights would awaken me . . . tiny eyes in the next room . . . clasped her unfamiliar hand . . . I would not give it nourishment. That morning was there. In my arms she tore back her yearning and pulled me to my feet. Speech contracted in circles, and I understand nothing except this thing.

Turning away her face from us stood watching that kicking baby. We began in a station and met swept clean across the plains. She followed her silence in every direction, calling down the wind and the rain accusingly. Her eyes swooped upon its prey: I did not weep.

She grew stronger, tightly about me, my body between them. Tangled in the folds and had laughed herself into solemnity. To me her living the same way made theirs—more rights over body and soul—pledged by such things to self-respect and conviction. We would go there—my voice continued—into a world.

A woman arrived in town with palm trees on the shores. The network of light—of tracks—regarded her with surprise. "Is there a train due here?" "You're too early," and vanished from her face. Hunger wondered if she could stand on her feet; every word uttered about her sought its way to food. She went away ethereal and almost pleasant. The wind in the tree far back recorded the floor.

Now long afterward my legs trembled when I stood. We talked of that intellectual world where waves of thought sweep for the depths, of work and nearly starved, of resentment downstairs, travel farther, weeping women, the eastern sky passing the dawn through material things. In a canyon, flowing by my bones, the river cooled.

The trail had guarded these rugged hills, black, stony, frying. Her head touched the ground in greeting, where the trees began to grow again. Into an arroyo and came up on the other side. At dusk the giant cacti, arms against the sky. Where the wind haunting the mountain captured her penetrated friendship. In the center, the string around, she was crossing over, changing places; the peculiar fierce movements of her body beneath me tore through the air. Neck to neck, the wind sweeping her hair back, lathering, rearing and whirling; through her muscles and her lips I received the quivering water.

IV.

Slowly the train came toward me, I heard her teasing voice. My face, my eyes, my skin and hair, moved forward. "I made them," then I turned and watched her. Voices here and there, heavy sleep, across the darkness we lay there, "this life couldn't stand you", or "I couldn't stand this life." I used to be strong . . . going to get work . . . died away uncovered and lay staring through the window. The watching stars seemed good or bad. Far up in a slumber a figure endured experience.

They told me what they believed, now you tell me who did that. The rich are interested in prostitution; let any man judge my nobody body. In my work her head blossoms and bent, a woman actively doing something. Dark and silent were the mansions who live and sleep in peace and luxury—they dug him out and his mouth was filled with mud. Belief and reason went again to the circle.

Little dried-up dances could reply to such arguments. I have learned and become a force, and the tea in my cup became cold. Before the sun comes up invaders mingled their customs. Their fragrance came to me with the shadow of purple skies, and the slender forefinger traveling across the page. I shall remember the past, perhaps the present, but the future dissected everything.

It has no fear, no money. Our heads were spreading, a touch of wistfulness in it. It comes back, as if I were a part of the air. Talk to me, I was a raw, impulsive woman, and work was intense. Let affection make conviction the basis of your action. I am organizing and fighting for the wind.

SAILED

Under a sky, in a garden, there are serious women and beautiful men, were talking. "You are much more beautiful," they implore, and can't help their red cheeks from flaming. "You are terrifying, too," and speak in the same voice.

He is already far away, is going to other trees on the horizon, disappear behind that cloud and drew around him closer a sleeping voice, lowered to a rolling feeling. In the dark she is sleeping, stroking on forever, buried in her hair this garden while the eyes of stupefaction widened, and the light curls lighting up this boy in the clouds would find him in some thick aureole covering her back and waking somewhere else . . .

I walk straight ahead, pays attention without always seeing, playing music the way I'd like to live. His lamentations would bring the cymbals together. I wanted to find out where they were enjoying themselves, followed them at a distance to where the beautiful nights dance like bears. I've remembered a cup of brandy, and went to sleep turned toward their faces, the stars.

From the air there was his eye in his forehead, the sun had a brother. One of them said, "Yesterday moves so slowly." One of them said, "Seemed to linger with pleasure in the great hollow sky." One of them said, "Each setting out in solemnity from a beautiful night like this . . . "

THE DEPOSITORIES

The enemy personified the nation. A fiction or series of fictions exploding through with smoke, pouring sweat. At the foot of a tree hands stuck in the dirt. Once in a while they hold on to me.

A couple of them seemed to be moving around the field, black-eyed, loose splinters from the neighborhood, full of wasted determination. He coughed it up on the pillow in a sort of puddle. The forms lying there, vacant, removed from there.

The house thin, blue, hanging in the air, transparent in the trees, the forms of the trees, no partition whichever way you move . . .

This man was weak, received a box from home, munching on a bloody cracker in the remaining hand. Two boatloads arriving, exposed to it anywhere, torches on the ground, rags around heads, hot at night with sudden energy, the maintaining skin of vengeance. Green oozing out from the grass—large spaces swept over—burning the dead beards, odor of the rejected arm and leg. In history the paper remain and still remain, soaking up the glaze . . .

I sit by his shining hair, the heart of the stranger. His ashy eyes, roasted in the morning. As you pass by, be on guard where you look. Opposite my window the freed horses are led off. The smoke streams upward, dark, thick, warm.

He said, "Make your own choice." The kiss I gave him discharged better views.

The man is struggling for breath; a soldier's life must be a bent thing. Others are arranged in a straight row. They have some old magazines I was in the habit of reading: theory, practice, democratic premises, superfluity. He was an ideal of his age in a few days. He kept a diary and wrote, "The doctors have been brave."

I am taking care of a silent rebel, laid down on his arm to see its distribution, lying on the spot that time a hole in the air, his small calculations extruded. Meat might be named from mere demonism; nature and pretense were there.

I like to stand and look a long while. Individuals in human places verify the forms. The dim leaden members with heads leaning and voices speaking. In the arms and in the legs from my observation.

Dear Madame, I have seized the testimony, still alive. I do not know his past life, but feel as if it must have been good. I saw circumstances, and can give you some fragmentary physiognomy and idioms . . .

Flesh of his breast and tremulous arms in the strain of a partial sleep, I have a special friend. Out of the shadowy scene the white beds, sat by a huddled form, shone in through the window a vacant moon . . .

Buttons . . . tufts of hair . . .
In bushes, low gullies, or on the sides of hills . . .

INSCRIPTION

Dear:

Tell me what the first name is. I've seen pictures, but the title you gave me isn't the one I meant. I suppose I wonder if you understand such a book—that landscape with its clay sky and still purer roofs. Every evening looks early in the morning, springing up into our whole body of light. His wings father other people in the things of everyday life.

We took a walk through corn fields as tall as a house, grey branches and black bushes of stones, the wind from the little white path blooming the wallflowers, and below the horizon projecting far into the sea. On the roofs of the houses I thought of you, not because I deserve it but because years cover all things. Goodbye to their parents which the boys wave from the window.

I would also like you to see the dark stairs with the rotten floor, and spend a winter with them in the past an oil stain on your drawing. A little word is sometimes how you are.

When I think of the past, or rather my evil self, and the virtuous eyes of so many other treasure ships, or rather photographs, I bring forth out of their treasure things these things, or rather the room shedding itself . . .

If I could work and not come back from where one has a view over the whole city, turnips, vines, roads, horses, drivers, I can follow the impossible lessons at a convenient distance and come out renewed. The path becomes a picture little by little;

passers-by see only a bit of smoke. Those trees you see protect you, and the memories gather all under that one name.

I said to myself, "Shall I be here?", but he says to me, "You'll recover." So I left him a few masterpieces, and he said, "I have already seen too many inconveniences."

I have already written like strawberries in spring. With my realism secrets initiate me into the palette. Afterwards, the brains with the hands chose the active part of this homesickness.

Write to me soon without my always being conscious of it. Don't forget I like thick paper that wakes me up in the night. It's in the air—something that can't stand the light. I sent you a drawing of the open air—my hands just can't keep from working!

This is my ambition of such and such a person it is not the language of nature. You'll see from the outline the composition is shifting. Such a position can go forward or back through some opening, look through it, it is absolutely the thing—aside from a few other things.

I would give you the impression we saw leaves in the wood, shadows blotted streaks in the glow by the trees. From the ground those black stems wandering around the dark masses, that dark ground of red, yellow, white. The trunks were clotted and rooted in the light because it is impossible. Something has spoken to me that can't be deciphered. The bushes are standing there.

Yours,

SPINNER

There is not a tree around; on the other hand there's an open invitation. The bird is not yet extinct as he flies his sorrows to sour peaches too far to walk.

We went slowly in the small air, a humming here and there; he spoke passing his hand over his thin eyes, and he looked at me without a trace of character. His attitude was one of supervision on the threshold of the half-open door. I admired his face of the evening sky—invades the warm body and closes the eyes, glow in the motionless hay, spring water, taking away . . .

Next day I paid a call on old-man broad shouldered himself. The same little eyes engaged me in conversation. When he did so, I was conscious of a feeling that I was not really right. Below his breath I asked him, "Sir, shall I spend the night here in your shed?"

"You'll be welcome!" he shouted, I threw myself down on the sweet-smelling sheet. Behind him his sons came in one after the other. I was absorbed by my new acquaintances, their confidences, and lived from mouth to mouth; his protection was endowed with advantages to cure frenzy or bleeding, had the touch, and makes his way instinctively creep out to meet him. The bird after which he is named is completed.

"Is it the same way there?" I would exclaim. "Tell us, sir, how is it?" I can't tell you all the questions, but he doesn't mind undergoing the future, as if it had been carved out of mammoth skin. He would accompany himself on the balalaika, shut his eyes in the grass smells and sing: “We drove off, the sunset was just beginning . . . “

THE PLACE

One will take a model for them and become plastically concrete. The conversation sees the words when they want to. Those walks or this figure will come out of most things, but that doesn't mean it's natural. There's a head—how beautiful it is!—if I may call it so. As for me who has eyes it's doubly stimulating, because I'm sitting here in silence—and then to swallow oneself as one is in order to sit down and rest . . . !

A phase of life isn't over then, but one begins more clearly. I feel a power of color, and wonder how it will develop. The clouds of the grass, for instance, when I look at them—that isn't called correctness, or the patches of raining road he felt by a person—himself evidently—while now we can talk it over also suffered in the story. Such calculations don't intend emotion or difficulties; everything is simplified in so far as it's not chaos.

When I say I have my everyday life, everyone must decide for himself. If things had happened the mere suggestion of the thing would occupy a certain rank in my own people. A simple word remains a wound and cannot be healed the first day. I hope you understand what battle this was.

So it is here, inside that evening sky, dark as a cave, most realistically. In order to give you an idea of the shape of a leg they stand in the gardens; on many faces they look faded from nearby, very faded. Narrower strips of color imagine the horizon. The sky covered the sky.

That same spot, if one works, becomes light. What I wanted to say is that we could walk here together.

WORLD

That day reality—and by no man of earth—was going out to be hunted. At moonset—his chief seat—he woke there. He couldn't see anything.

This forest is thick; that must be why several women evoking pleasant images soon faded. She followed it; the quarry must have changed its course. He stopped. This place can't be a right place. Before his eyes bodies colder than snow leapt over him.

It was moving, it was coming—wish it was something else—of a wind at the stranger unbidden—what is it?—glint of carcass in the deep voice—our world is one—he understood—forced upon him in which all things took shape, form after form among us because we make room. He looked hard at the trees—they burned through his skull—"Tell me what to do and I will do it."

Shape will be on you, neither a man nor my queen—he has arts—he looked down and saw hands shaped like hands. A heaving might have torn loose the warm young flesh he was used to. I will have his things—walking away from yourself—and he will have mine.

The musicians were keeping time as if they were being made by one Thing. He saw it, but he was too late. When they found him, a great black scale fell to the earth.

They were in a wood of her tales. She sat whittling leaves. The wind glittered like foam. It seemed real.

A great bird descends from the sky.
Its beak gleamed in the red light.
Through them poured the cool breeze.
The birds have dreamed me beneath the apple trees.

IN THE MIST

On Monday the window was open; the night followed me and couldn't be quieted. I smoked at the sky, lay down in the rain—blind devotion—for a person mirrored in the sea the sky is melodic.

He was a man—(fear the awakening)—a woman—(my lovers passed in illusion)—I rode in a forest—(religious instinct?)—opened the exaggerated sun—a kind of sweating lassitude.

I lie on my couch—everything has changed—patience of the mists—pump into the entrails of things—he sucks up sunlight, pounding with joy, precise as a cello. Someone comes along and separates me from the form. Evangelical milk and humanitarian thighs and socialist drapery. It's not enough to have wings; when I unfold them your perfume rises from the paper.

Great stretches of water—a gray vapor that appears to be moving—sunset melted dark ink—mass of trees—my ministerial partition—with the space of days before an address. As dancers ripple and retreat their faces remain movements of a body.

I thought of her dance without meaning, whistling through the bushes. My feet ahead of me—one among others—trembling resources—between that enormity and the moon on the hilltop here. Now I can hear part of myself penetrated by individualities. The city is immense.

This changeable sky sees the buildings differently. There are more flowers in the house than in the ground. The floor a forest of dark olive trees, sea at the far end . . .

Shadows glide beyond the plains with white sails—almost in the air—moving noiselessly over the surface of things. Another ocean climbed the mist, adjusting that human anatomy: horizon lines. I forget what I stayed at home to do. The blue spread out.

With my elbows on the table I'm going back to that place.

from UNBOUND: A BOOK OF AIDS

HUMAN IMMUNE

I lie in your arms. I kiss your mouth. Use your nails, creature. Our roles—the crown, the infractions—inhabit this sanctified place to the point of fanaticism. I have to get my hands on the world.

Dead from complicity in San Francisco discharged me, the harp of a person had an arc. Then listen to inhale the contagion, where in the trap of your consciousness you have to pull to get out. Himself alone and scared kill mercies. The body has powers to paint yourself purple.

And shifting grasses, such erosion and mosses, nightjars lived on the droppings of sunny days . . . in that country of circumstances and moods—shattering its bark and throwing pieces of it around. Facing away from the entrance, with jerky movements kicking the sands backwards. I saw the size of a hand, losing hold of it . . .

Birdmen, across the rising hills and bay, rolling naked one night stirred and rose to the spell. He's out there, into the dead stumbling mind. I'll be accounting for no memory, without so much as a template. His nostril is hissing; his tongue in spasms. He has several parts on a breeze, an asylum this story surrounded. The face ripping wide open has led a team of men in white gowns and slow rhythm.

And twinges we ourselves devise woundingly by miscalculation—delicious conflagration winking—to become familiar and to pulverize them all. Curves could hope to find in this world no more beautiful hair. *Hell is round.* I squirted them with kisses. On his back at the edge of the couch to die of pleasure, kneeling into your asshole to form around me. Comprise our friends the memory of the moments they passed in that virtue. Their honor therein, helpless before desire . . .

Where are you now, the harder you pull to get out? Then is that person fixing little sandwiches and watching TV? The Bay was fucked—ornate theories—there's the previous photo of "husband", hippies, Pt. Reyes beach, leering face, pink light, someone else. A portion of scripture, undiagnosed. The placement of objects is a language theme, no longer private. A little old hairless man had swollen up. Pain is healing me into submission, he wrote in his journal the secret of the universe: *hell is round.* You flop and thrash in fact.

The homecoming was marked and mapped; they circled in ever widening loops. Processions migrating on blue nectar—stopping in the rising air over coastal waters. I waited I repeated I waited the test. The results were not fooled. I spent the summer as a natural landmark—the bearer of delicate organs—leaving the destiny dormant on dry days—moving my wooden ship to research, under spell of the spray. The sun was gigantic, slow, low-hanging. We had to acquire some knowledge in this year, food for a narrative. Summer is short. Inquiry raising our eyebrows was contagious. Moonlight on meat.

He knelt down next to me—fallen giant, empty stump. Feeling the blood pulling around my thighs, "I think it's screaming," I said.

He stood barefoot, one warm leg, nest at the belt, pink wriggling sack, I wanted to run into the sun now, bristling muscular bulging animal sedated by his eyes. My body shook against him on a hot summer day, gushing to life, blood-filled, blood-dizzy. He rolled over onto his side, watching the men. A ruin. A patient. Overgrown so that the flat air had no answer. We floated in which the memory moving our bellies going dark have all taken flight—a cure may be possible—tell me what words mean—pleasure for a coffin: turn and enter your home.

The ghost which leads to burning incense on the altars of magical friends—these gods come upon gods which erects them—confections of the deific—showers down events, the smooth operations of insignificant romances to penetrate into their historian's hearts and foist upon the reader authenticity of the marvels . . . At last he dies, this exceptional man who loves them, phantom spawn, fraudulent cures, boundless poverty and the images of objects. Just a while ago I gave you attentions pure and simple. I take the oath worthy of your friendship exterminated in me. The lancing pain stuffing me with bucks and thwacks to distill soul's fuck: slip away, leave the rest to me, initiated into our mysteries . . . .

With the Sixties the Seventies in Berkeley shot forward for replay to put the spaces where he wants—stars in the universe suggest metaphysical poets—lingered in remission studying the cosmic characteristics of T-cells. Triumphant skull in the grin of his malady, whacked as he was in a feedback loop. It's necessary to interpret men compared to sleepers in a private world. Two men pass through a forest which passed for the real world. From the cardiac ward through the underground corridor to encounter arrhythmia on the cathode screen. His head, his heart, a wave-form. And he spoke his monologue directed outward from the wisdom of a body: *hell is round*, the little clay pot locked up. The dream-time of heroes trying to throw up names: California, Parsifal, Chuck . . .

Night fell and a moon showed up between peaks. We were given a welcome for centuries. Aroused by smell in their human behavior a growl in heat, with a mixture of affection and respect. A little whipping, a little touching it lightly. One sometimes hears the ice snap with a seam in the center; large numbers breeding in our district at those breathing holes. Members kill themselves, interested only in sugar. Suddenly the door was flung open, a youth tumbled in; the event we'd been preparing for changed our life entirely. To wake up to stop the alarm clock with one hand I lay on my right side facing my other—my Other Side—pressing the human places in a firm grip that woke us up in horizontal posture turned to face each other, covered with a thick blanket, the murmur of description, connected by an invisible rod as resistance fluttered back and forth.

The end of perspective, the proper shapes, blobs and pillars and singing minarets. You're a mess in the park. You're a willing dirty dog. With the sun disappearing a low fog tucked-up the air. I slept resting on the windowsill, stranger than birds. I used to be little but when we came back they were gone. Overnight to hear whatever was to be heard. With its overgrown boxed body jerking in perfect symmetry, this wizard—see what there is to see—bruised in deep breaths, and an archaeologist invited down to watch. He'd like to go from the bay to the ancient golden hills into the earth unannounced and never saying where. It was like some mechanical body secretly unstrung leaving accretions of soft dirt and mud. He kissed his waiting hand with both hands. The warm competence of the finished parts as if such machines had meaning. Touching it, the thin shell, tucked-in facing the bay may lie quiet in the dusk.

A way is opened; my initiated companions go after. Each gave his confrere the pleasure of sensations, sprawled on the stone floor. Sucking a moment of suspense into calm to savor its entirety, the combination of prick and ass and mouth, an eternity in that delirium he'll lie in your arms. Common measure in homage to fitting company. We'll make a circle (*hell is round*), I want that energy while speaking, place yourselves close by me, excessive behavior swell discourse in proportion, the carnal prosperity of an everyday affair. It ripens and is born, having provided circumstances. Made an incision running around the head, then removed the strip of skin. Your body, the altar, on the altar. Go consult the children of love. There are minds, my friends, certain spirits, having rid themselves of vibrations, having progressed from extravagance to the speeding star, plagued in whose name passion alone dared multiply. Come—this'll serve as a bed—fuck my ass into my mouth.

This is what the dream referred to as *hell is round*. When he got out of the hospital it had the effect of wiping out history. Right now, the city was in intensive care, locked-out behind him. In the small room huge eyes flaming. His fried mind projecting on each side a sword to conquer—through the sense organs through the rain through the ward through the trembled fields of flowers as if shape had no substance through the living information completing itself. The blood of communion turning is a strange sentence. It broke through and fired experience at his head. Penetrated man penetrated himself. He was dragged through his address book deconstructed as official documents—the only way open. A limbo in lymphoma contemplated itself: he lived it, he loved himself, would love that too. He saw it spread out among us, pulled from his body. He could hardly wait to abolish himself, freeing him to go commando saving people, glommed onto another pretext in grief and love through the magical powers that underlay all his saved-up strategy . . .

I have variations about what was there: fathers, sons, and grandsons. When the sky cleared the weather superimposed corrections, noticing and recording more details. Fly to an elevated lookout post. It's my intention to describe history at the place we left them. Populations of flesh caught in our net. Of their courtship, of their species: their back was connected to display-movements fading toward the warm neck, a pirouette. Small circles this ceremony for hours on end. About the organization of behavior: some of them visited me. Animal behavior in the summer of 1956, or '76—embarrassing luxury—while we were floating on the shore or in the sea or under veils in quiet corners as the haze hanging behind us . . . Feverish outburst played havoc with their exact pose while sitting indoors, digging out of the morning for tests, returned positive results on the same day; distance . . . I've made a number of flights already—round flat discs—homing. Then my legs stopped moving altogether. Under the full microscope ferocity with nerve endings waiting I hovered, motionless, maneuvered into position.

I will see him standing, pounded, irresistible. In the dunes of my thick woolen sweater, dropped off along the western edge, panting through the indistinct sand, puncturing the middle of the farthest horizon, arms raised. Through the muscles of aching arms and legs opening on my back to the sea, wrapped in tangled sunlight staring beyond him. What I didn't think or say fill my mouth, the terrible mysteries of sleep and navigation. We're best friends ever since ever. I noticed you in class—my full attention—if given the opportunity stammering to encompass love stanzas. Have you smiled?—choreography! Are you wrapped around my waist?—cosmic winds. San Francisco the beauty can take a picture—the air around him. I lay there on the floor, dug into the trenches, throwing down his trousers, the root of bones and mud and blood. I suppose he once lived here, curled into the tails of my nightshirt. He walked past me in his undershorts, an organism. We are the owner of sight and speech. In the gray light west of the Great Highway: not even me. We sat in silence, a blanket covering his lap. If you flew by you'd see these imposters, vapors of tenderness. It could never be contained.

from A DOOR

THRESHOLD

I listen every ten seconds to the dahlias—birds in a nest—and little by little recognize the road in the distance, smaller, scattered into words, competent. On the table a cloudy glass is distinguished from its ring on the napkin by regular intervals coiled in place.

Militant home life—localized pleasures—can't be interpreted through the window. Significance is on the pink wall with irregular pulsations of light. A little cloud of dust stops for a moment outside the door straining at its hinges.

Your comrade—my struggling body—is banging against the skin of a drum. Those songs flush the milky blueness out of insomnia. The skin of the wing vanishes through sleep or consummation.

You wrote, and the loops of that stream impatient to roam the world were pushing some detail into place: she rubs herself with coconut oil. She stood on tiptoe, covered with sun. She laughed sprawling in cotton shorts full of moist sand.

His head resting on his folded arms—easy familiarity—warm path—shower of petals—as the round shadow dropping from a lamp will soon dissolve in light— hesitated and spoke, absolving the upturned trees.

His roving eyes streamed down the shore, adding maturity as I wiped my neck in the presence of detachment. When we dive we keep our unexpected eyes open. A stroke of work. A fragment of homage capable of moonlight.

Will you be warm enough? In the shape of a body a drama of gestation communicated themselves to me. The eucalyptus air—electric moths—is striking a passing car. Her bare arm and the incomparable scarf drive on through that corolla.

The rising landscape—gesture of rain—watched them trickling down. Then rubbed with that sea my house smokes, taking the wind away from the present without looking back. You remain on the threshold between us to fill my cupped hands.

RIDERS

I wore them because the smell of saliva on them had parallel with their bodies. Once you were in those wings you knew all you needed to know about preadolescent blue pajamas. I lay in bed sleeping and waking, salt and pepper. Hairs made me feel grown up.

When anyone spoke of my cousins I was watching a figure emerge sideways—long expanse of his back tearing up the kitchen—expelled prickly sweat as my knee against—pulled the cinch tight till it flew like streamers behind me.

He'd written the text on his body I pulled a book from the shelf into my private mythology. I'm in a downtown hotel. He comes to visit us. I was scolded. Glances of the old men. I was undressed beside the public pool. The restrooms holiday three sons friendships quick hug narrow hips stay over living room couch enormous poppies confidante clutching my hand between the doorway and the bed.

All identification had been long forbidden and secured. I sat in a chair in the accounting of simultaneous feeling. Diverted from refusal as inevitably as ill-prepared, by some quirk of natural ability through dark brown eyes. He is my music, a box of pastels, draped kimono, red vase, linen sheets, falcon fate, epitaph, sailor, short pants, fish smell, rhyme word, Italian sonnet, spin cycle, black grease, ball point, back stairway, towered wall, hotel room, my bookcase I'm lying on the couch my field of daffodils I put my empty lips against his until my eyes are swollen shut, his shoulders pinned me, smell of neck hair and dog smell—tell me how to breathe—one of their own—tight around our legs—older than we were . . .

". . . their tangled manes by force of wind
aslant from their extended necks . . ."

FIN DE SIÈCLE

It's as though the wandering sky I knew whose gliding companions mimic the clouds seemed to be watching its reflections in the window—I'll dream of kisses—making my thoughts hang and ripen into cities. O you underworld arsenals, days split their flowering skin of tremendous fields—the grandeur of my poses pure mirrors—towards the rival sun. I'm imperfect in my floating perfumes and delirium. I love memory.

Who whose smooth invitation fattened up by fertility goes spreading under the polished sky classical lessons—it was summer—and made the tolling blaze at the end of the corridor drink space—the body was alive and multiplying—penetrating image of the year a sun lies on anything that is green. I was lamenting winter.

When I breathe my nostrils people the dark world that is absent with human reposes. There came a frame—it be the work—in which myself with frowning eyebrows give you appearance—then you lay under my destiny as a river sheds hot water. I love a man choked like a forge. I believe you open the door from fear alone.

In those times that sun lodged in him are one flaming hillside—pouring essence on the floor—and the shivering falsetto paintings flourish in his simple studio. Afterwards, the metaphysical skies will be heavy with farewells.

It is, despite his meditating efforts, slanting winter. Girl of swishing tatters and men are making the clouds tinkle. Banging himself and stumbling under the suspended sky he was not a temple but high in their midst. I, whose memory was once entrancing, was standing in allegory and smeared with my own image. The wincing sky, all its entrances exits. In the enemy sky, soup of streetlamps and bedrooms.

They say I'm submerged through those mirrors, windows, and draperies. None of these things can equal the tender sky. You make me think of sweeping boas, thud of summer light, slumber jars. Pillow sabbath. Opium labyrinth. Foaming bread or wine.

O and on things the morning in parallel-beam glides towards the sun and hardens. It was in the past, double, of an afternoon bliss—one of those recitals—and which you feel yourself coming to shaped like a crown.

Someone appears; the slower atmosphere of significant gravity.
You are my equal. Take me away, filled with appetite and infancy.

THE LAST HEAD I PAINTED

In comparison with different people, whose lives some people can draw conclusions from, my body is no immediate speculating attack. I came after an endless voyage after they approach the horizon. This excursion is full of what I've seen, which exactly gives that effect: the compact sky shows great hulks in the evening. One is overwhelmed by things—silent from the window—where you find huts and the living room—what tranquility—where I am now, that dark room, from an open door, collected; things adjust themselves.

Follow that little point between the green weeds and corn. I scratch memory: it has the same eyes they had. Without metaphor the same apple was or was not a thing.

Lamplight—which has light *in* it—will speak vaguely about the colors that have no name. Last week I saw a hesitation much greater than literal truth.

All that architecture, the sky, is calculated in one rush; in the corner individuals are walking. For instance you are walking, with pearl-grey eyes, in the open air, expressing what I want . . .

PELE'S SMILE

The pattern is local, with detailed information (free love) and that light upon the body from the nearest star: Immensity of Itself.

In the pantheon of months the boat sails under excessive heat—it sailed beyond him—that summer of confidence and compromise—with one hand playing a melody over one hand that still dreamt of going there. The friendship between his gauzy brightness and the aureole of the sun blazed on (love was free) and the sails flapped on the horizon: Community of Spirit.

On Monday their moans could be heard drifting across the wind. I pluck the golden crown to make a toy boat—and gaze back at the receding shore. They laughed with the unfolding water: Maternity of Trust.

RED GERANIUMS

She had an errand in town, put on her hat to reflect the clouds passing. At lunch, hooded with childlike exultation—plateful of green pleats—the allure of soup—she thought about subject and object, respect for wife and children, disliking dogs, and abruptly observed the wallpaper.

Her bird alight on the line like that—the living plank in the picture—quivering freak admiration—transferred the anguished rain of energy to equilibrium. She gave these exaggerations the burden of pure joy.

Tablets bearing inscriptions achieve intimacy; her tribute reduced a shadow to good faith. Grope children world power paint-box—an old woman with red cheeks drinking soup repeated the words "I'm the king."

and I at night with a gentleness corporeal minced around in my visible skin before the protective window like a damp rag against the pink sky—spin away from their borders into blankets, flames, the future spewing the past on my chest or ass. I jumped up and paced the room—it was *mine*—collecting a thing of beauty comparable to mountain peaks, the metaphor of my flying solitaire. Excitation at four in the morning is a philosophy class.

I went out loving even my roommate, delirious with attention to work, weavings, other people's ideas, drinking romantic coffee, featuring me physically wedged in the sphere.

My life had material facts! (weightless!) and phantasmagoric phrases (skull!). On a bus I even thought of my parents. The droopy heads thrilled me about achievement and excellence. Every chair had a heaviness from which sprang rationality and passion—with my body proximity communal, cortex wave.

It was Sunday afternoon in a building arranging my clothes—streaming necklace—surrender the flowers to the wind—the intimacy of milk cartons—mutual corona—a concentrated cigarette in an ashtray on the glass table.

repose in anonymity the concrete landscape
"ravishment of the intellect by coming nearer to the fact"

LITTLE MADRIGAL

I know nothing. These are things in themselves—obscure plaster; evacuation matter—the night at his feet of which the reporter was to interrogate.

I saw him coming and my heart beat so fast the metamorphosis was on the tip of my pen. Little madrigal—leaped up and said: "The entire outer world listens, weighed down by personal interest. But hotly, and proofs exist." He opened his door to embellishments and revealed himself better.

But shame, punishment, mercy make us leap to the skies—I kiss your hands plotting out the acts and scenes—all the submissiveness such a great fall requires. It makes me shudder, this peril, so drink to my health. The trouble with correspondence is more details.

JINNEE

One day which stood numerous—a great wooden trough—passengers paddled with my eyes until resigned to myself closed in.

One day in the distance as I drew nearer a man emerged from the ground each month and questioned me: "What's the restitution, and when will you come hide in our hiding places?"

One day my absence dissolving climbed into a tall tree: a cow, a buffalo, an elephant, elephant fat, apes, locusts, a black fur, camel lips, tore the body to pieces with his fingernails, a dog asleep snoring which filled our hearts with description, a donkey which resembled a cow and a sea-bird.

Seeing the violent world—eminent merchants—one day naked men with a strange ointment anointed their bodies. Their distended bellies reaching the rolling plains—go on across the grass to the opposite side. The markets and well-stocked shops gathered around to bid me farewell—I lay in a corner with a leg bone so that the ornamental air would come back with terror, and I was rapturously welcomed.

One well-trained day dragged out the young bird. The sun weighed anchor in the ominous twilight, crouching upon my shoulders, one foot against my belly, kicking me every time I stopped. After weeks of servitude I began to ferment, tripping around the trees so woozily I'm known among the travellers as 'Washed Ashore'. I ran to the edge of the tilting deck and said, "I'm a very old man.

I have been young and beautiful and the men grew wings on their shoulders and for

One day flew in the air—all his possessions my possessions—to allow me to cling to him took hold of his waist carried me up swiftly into the high higher . . . I saw two faces coming up towards me. 'Who are you?' 'We are your worshippers.' 'Is this how friends behave?' 'We are the bonds of friendship.' Leading him away the boys kissed him again and again with tears running down his cheeks. "Mother," he cried, "that man is my other mother." It would be a grief or a wealth in his need. *I am here, master—I am here at your service!*

from INVOLUNTARY LYRICS

INVOLUNTARY LYRICS

I.

If the judgment's cruel
that's a wake-up call: increase
energy, *attention*. These little pumpkins ornament
themselves with swells, die
pushing live volume packed spring-
form hard as a knock: Decease
and resist. Content
surges exactly as memory
closes its rear-guarding
eyes
— the world rushes *in* not *by!* just be
steady, receptors, measure is fuel:
whatever moves move with the
drift which moving never lies.

III.

San Francisco, ah, west
of ascension, none of us wanted posterity
before we got to pleasure it! Another
sick, sickening, the
last newest
in his prime.
You, for all of us came crawling through dim alleys to mother
and shining see
even if still we're trailing in and out of city's womb
calls us and too discharges time
alone inside our tender bodies—dry,
do, my still-seeing eyes; nightmare's made me raise my fearful
head again. Be
extravagant meaningful polis, clearful sky, the
really it has been loving gesture of light undoes the tomb!

VII.

Everyone around's having 50th birthdays, pilgrimage
markers, up in Bodega Bay light
grayed above cliff face, distant seals' bark, so far yet so clear, car
of evening riding in with billowing cape: another metaphor for
  age? Oy! The eye
that should have met mine didn't, reversed from that day
troubles friendship subterranean unspoken such complications, sight
uneasy forward from backward lit, are
we then in this stupid majesty
both lost and found or in *and* out or on *and* off our way?
On the hill
with moon-pod wild thistles, shaggy, noon
seeming midnight in their spooky glare, we met, climbing, three age-
marked walkers, 70s I guess, caustic, bright, two women pals and
  gentleman poet. I
might've been son.
The throaty ducks shut up, we introduced, locked eyes, really
  there is mutual pleasure,
wind-silvery eucalyptus leaves and their pentagram nuts
  suspended, still.

VIII.

I come to café I sit, I bear
my part in the general cruise. One, sadly
won't look at me, another
won't look away; ridiculous assumption and snarled consumer joy
in abeyance, ordering
quotidian life according to compulsions or ordered by, focus
    shifting but always
aligned. Well, gladly
I'd mother
that guy with a stubble but he wants a father. I won't annoy
his diligent linearity. Man I just yesterday had sex with in park—sing
muse—said "Yum" and somehow knew to pull my head on his
    shoulder, little bleating sounds.
One heart, one mind, one chance but right now one
second's second chance he just walked by this café walkman in ear
real time I could've run and, what, left the poem? Composition
    deems none
such interruption permissible; shit, the sheer complexity
    confounds.

XIV.

the eyes
of cruising Dante named threading, stellar
compass to pass this way have done
with me or you, heart
warming literal your hands on me
held
sun
so art-
fully the
skill
employed rub down heat from on high art
hand lies
over heart
contain clamorous overbeating still

XLI.

On my log perch in the park—finally sun prevailed
after weeks of rain—commits
one's eyes to color, a certain sheen, bare
before light or clothed in light, heart-
shaped clover fluffs up, dew drops play globe, stinky acacia's
    blooming youth-
like glandular smell befits
a day seems young, randy even which turns it toward luscious
    age—so there
in vivid distance one sees Mt. Diablo as attainable, San Fran-
    cisco itself a perch or point of view, high art's
mental cartography, plum blossoms pinking the air. Truth
won
for clear light a city diversity grandeur cliff's edge the
giddy flight over moaty Bay or endless imagination Pacific
    assailed
by wave froth and fog dramatic but not veiled so pure Northern
    light prevails, "true" visual light on me
now right side cleared and raised in heat besotted devoted son.

LI.

Dear *leptospermum*, tiny magenta flowers on needly branches,
    please know
I meant no offense
mistakenly conflating you with AIDS-related intestinal disorder
    cryptosporidium—the pace
of vocabulary assimilation is mocked by speed
of exfoliating information dropped in saturated brain. I know
    well your floral twinkle made
of sober contrast and mistook you in name only; raise, then,
your superior modesty my way again, please. In race
last night to spy through window at street disturbance nervous need
proved careless I broke favorite yellow vase with rain-like slashes
    on it jaded
in my hurry to control, find
out the source of someone else's noise. You hearty desert flower slow
down my attention as you must slow
infrequent rain, I'll go
absorbed more cautiously your small determined face in blustery
    wind

LIX.

A man's (sic) just a shell enclosing a pulsating tooth; mine
abscessed is done
governing me, is
gone, a hole. Say
I'm beguiled
by that frame
of nothingness, *not* a hole *a gum* yet "tooth" still rules searching
tongue, a miss
more active than a hit. Proust-body that parts maintain the parts they
were a child
holding tooth in hand the same man contemplates a dream of
pillow, the same
contract with pain, the same open look.
Then let me sleep for days
or a life, sun
on my face upraise-
d a shell surrounding a hole, a tooth in a book

LXXI.

tomorrow, whoa,
I'll be dead
this verse
'll be the bell
that rings me clay
my feet have fled
rehearse
my some kind of shape — it dwell
right here decay
stinky but mine not
yet but not not moan
beginning so
far away for me who will have been gone
coming from where I'll forget, I forgot

LXXIII.

a red lamp in the green of the night rest
head on his chest be hold
tight by him on fire
or hang
from neck as lie
like vertical weight off cold
toes warming day's breath expire
where he sang
through lungs by
breathing day
go or night come strong
in silence this west-
ern shore house bed with him on long
that trail away

LXXXVII.

He was swerving
toward me on that road for my possessing
though him not knowing
how to estimate
—*I* did—the charge of the encounter—*fate* did—mistaking
for casual and so releasing
what was already growing
independently, indeterminate
to his eyes but—*I* knew, making
sure to water, granting
sunlight, flatter
circumstance with psychic tropism deserving
his further attention intrigued and the matter
of the fact now finds me getting his kisses I was wanting!

XCI.

The best
of all possible words would skill
the poorest harper a.k.a. me
whom the magisterial force
has raised above the cost
of materials, I mean experience, which'd make me ill
if I didn't have courage to be
a wimp and give the horse
my head. It boast
on my behalf the little bearer of pleasure
in glorious guise multiplicitous who take
from heave and rest
the pulse to make
measure

CXXII.

Clearing the mist
of language in temperament one has like flowers brain
on a stem hold
together memory
and number to score
days remain
quixotic and bold
the experiment leaks toward eternity
as if more
blood were pulled from heart
than *in* the
streaming then nova subsist
of pinhole me
as stars part

from CITIZEN

COOL DUST

A heave of afternoon light pulls a tulip from the turf, a bower for locusts, a cup of shells. The farmhouse tilts, a bent shadow on wheels. In cedar rooms a family is molded, silent, wrapped in the wire of steel eyes and stopped voice, romantic ash. This is not my house, my ghost, my uninvited guest, my lost labor of love, my thicket or grease, my JPEG gessoed or rawhide suit. The yellow light throbs like an internal organ—soft body of an overture to insect sounds—sapling of a new world—whose future awaits me at the tilting window of my own domestic hut. Perhaps this is my mesh of hours, my muscular ache, my guardian sash, twist of rope carved around an old maple trunk, my rod of power red with anticipatory friction at the edge of an emerging set of planetary rings. Stained ochre by the air I pitch forward, a vanilla-scented pear that floats or falls. In the rattan chair on the front porch by the blistered boards of the front door a figure of tar watches. Cool dust sparkles and settles. Shadows have made me visible. An empty wagon flares on the hillside.

POSITIONED

A thought without a body is not a star. The yellow house in spring behind the yellow leaves, as if the sun meant to land there, squeezed between gray walls like a trap-door, an exit sign . . . And so positioned as if the day itself had escaped the cartographer's lock she polished her eyes beside the windows—always windows and doors—and generated fractions—phrases, we call them—rain-filled hoof-prints and mica strands—refracted in the looming glass like a sphere shedding horizons. Who was her secret polar tug, her bell pull, her Adam cup? Was she raising or lowering ladders inside the staggered light, head down as if in thought but seeing the mounted sky; the peeling, corrugated bark; the coppery cigarette butts and polished plywood table tops and dripping mugs of ale, lit up like sunset gulls bound on the dive . . . ? Did she shiver in the shower of filaments themselves shivering, flared up in the corners and planes where they fell and streamed for her mouth and ears? The body of my star is a thought she plucks from the air that calls her name . . . astronomer . . . wholly intemperate . . . the chandelier of noon . . . her cheekbone perched on her index finger while the patterns spread . . . vibrating frame . . . giant wingèd brain . . . imminence

CONVECTION

For a day parsed into segments—woke at Yellow Awning, worked, ate lunch together through Medallion Aisles, worked hard, had a scotch or mescal at Diameter, studied, had a light dinner during Honeycomb, studied more or watched TV or read till we tucked ourselves into bed at Smoky Tendrils, or sometimes stayed up talking late into Slipping Staircase till we fell immobilized onto the blankets, glazed like burnt sugar . . . That story we are toting in our pockets and gums, our rolled up trouser legs and bouncy shoes, in our ageing elbow and knee creases—red-faced finches and rising incense and an artifactual pulpit of carved copal with its salamander glyphs and distant spent volcano—as we shuck our greasy uniforms, stained from cochineal and chili paste . . . wavered at the apex of the hour in the liquored heat . . . we sweep the floor where the water jug broke and scrutinize the blinking shards . . . elaborated affinities . . . dust smell and gas fumes of the aged city by uneven foot down the close streets with syrupy air under great flowering clouds in the thick of bodies crammed into an afternoon swell on the heaving valley floor through visionary traffic snarls over rounded stones . . . thunderstorms there at the scrim of the hill every day advancing . . . our faces drenched as we rush for cover . . . crafted genealogies . . . our thunderstruck, silent, upturned faces drenched . . .

SAGACITY

Look at the past, that conduit of vapor—she squints at the window as if rummaging through time—mumbling something about "my body . . . "—patina flows—redistributed flank . . . Each morning as she works at her desk the cramped hand and its . . . or the influx of his muscular smile as he used to . . . a still point on a revolving globe, a spoon of hours . . . the little silver cat wiggled free of her lap, licked his stretched paw—(if she could lick her paw!)—and forgot the previously-to-die-for strokes . . . She got up and stretched as best she could, prickly fingers . . . an influx of where she was, the immediate coordinates of the sunlit room, ivory walls, sloping floor, baskets and painted pots, the open ledger, the notebook splayed like a specimen; a clatter to attention as if cramming down meatballs or toasted nuts or big fists of runny cheese, if she could seize them and fix them, if she could lock the melodious facts in place . . . She stood still in the gale of objects and signs like a mast, sucked at the wind, crossed her arms, stared down a yellow bowl, *dared* it to fade . . .

EL DESEO

Where did he go when he couldn't say—spire or plateau—when the elastic alphabet vaulted beyond his will or way—he wanted to—nomad with sand in his hair—he wanted to—tumbled in or out of bed with sleep in his eyes, moths winging—he wanted to—a litany of origins, crescendos, divagations, loose ends, open ends, signs and signposts—he wanted not so much to say as know how to say and what to say—in the hot groan of afternoon that pressed him in and jacked him up—floating but tethered—his flask of lips closed to himself but open to me—though he wanted to—hands raking my hair, whisk of his breath, amulet eyes, as the drawn yellow curtains fluttered and heaved and the pink walls flashed—I wanted to . . .

IN THE DOME

In truth it was the flask of the sky I put to my lips like a castaway, from the ridge of the patio lookout, palm fronds clashing, the salmon-stucco bellower with its great pendulous bell—I wanted to—and the clouds whisked across in flat sheets, streaming plateau, until suddenly the hot blue sky flares and the hot thick air falls with its litany of parrot screech, clanging gate, engine cough—I wanted to—where you can feel the still-restless, saturated turf shift underfoot, and wait for the great tumbling rain to free the next generation of buried moths in a whispered frenzy—plate shards and fabric shreds, moon-white pumpkin seeds and fluttering corn husks—I wanted not so much to say as be said to—rotating sonar . . . elastic alphabet . . . amulet ears—in the torrid mix of wind and dust and rusty guitar, a swirling vault of pressed voices, untold clasps—I wanted him to . . .

EDGE OF LIGHT

Where can you say or when can you say and who can you say it to—he nearly did—fragments of speech, nomad body parts tumbled on the verge—he needed to—moths in darkness, but floating towards—he couldn't yet—in the flamboyant heat that grilled him and which he sparked—knowing the gestures and moves—elastic innocence—but not the shape or how to punctuate—skidding origins—or that the women in the square and circling through the streets weighed down by piles of colored cloth strapped to their shoulders might not carry his name stitched there in silver thread, embroidered litany—he could almost—from the plateau of the unmade bed—a flask of tequila at hand to burn back the rising words—amulets each, but only if strung—his hands outseeing his eyes by miles—vaulted arches, quivering spires—and me breathing into his mouth, "You will, you will, you will . . ."

THE STILLNESS

Once I was a sailor in a town with no name—hey nonny nonny or go cat go—I had a red mountain bike and two skateboards—wheel confetti—but my skiff was my über-pal. I could split the seam of any vector—river, lake or draw—with coots sputtering from mangrove jumbles, surprised by my sudden proximity—and the imprint of my oar in the liquid sky barely visible . . . Some called me Mica Glint and some called me Mary Louise and both were fine with me, depending on which shoes I wore, sleek rubber or nubby hemp, woven in strips or knit from fallen leaves . . . I could cut through downtown squat in the slats, as low and clean as a needle . . . gravel showers parting . . . clattering, gray canyon air . . . Once I was a sailor with my long hair flowing, with a satchel of pink apples and a bouquet of peas, tendrils trailing . . . in a stub of an afternoon removed from sequence . . . heretic hovercraft . . . in a flat eddy where you watched from the shore or corner or car or chair . . . to whom I waved relentlessly as I glided past, uncoiling my way in circles or arcs such as cursive letters make . . . in that gap, in that rounded space, in my silent groove like a paper boy in a paper boat turning as I was turning . . .

COWBOY DON'T

Cowboy, don't eat me. Yes I'm tasty, yes I've come from my warren stuffed like a Christmas goose, tongue lolling. But cowboy, think of my varnished nose, my bucket of pink gums, the opera of my eyes. Let the knotted grid loosen, let your hard silhouette overflow—alluvial redemption—let me slink away soundlessly into the lavender hills—sanctuary caravan—cowboy, don't eat me, go for the calf over there, tender as cactus jelly. I'm too sweet and too fat, my innards are frescoes of hormone spikes and acid splats—*mucho* digestive scrabble—don't open me to the scouring winds, please, close your paring knife, your dripping cowboy lips . . . Life is episodic and a revolution idles, there behind the pink escarpment where my pack is gathering now . . . The world, *este mundo inmenso*, gyrates and kicks, and the hot stars *in their pale ignition* are burning . . . burning . . .

GLORIA MUNDI

Once I was an old man with wind in his hair—pulverized by the air—that wasn't fair so I crawled back over the bridge *to where the beautiful nights dance like bears*—and sidling up to the Professor of Youth who was seething to see me unspooled sat down in my former spot with a heft of purpose . . . and with my eyes now sparkling like fresh cream started to sing, "Attention purifies the vagrant mind" as if it had been peeled out of a hymnal from my childhood . . . Once I was a Young Turk with wind at his back—it was hard to argue with *that* . . . Once I had a tunic of cobalt blue, a twilight cape, a dark kimono . . . with a sweep of authority as if it were my hair I climbed the laddered air to where the voices hung like ornaments in cobalt space—dancing bears—and waited in the sonic arches as if I were at home there and learned my methods and honed my craft . . . Bridge and arch, ladder and stair . . . happily at home there . . .

THEN

Once we were in the loop . . . slick with information and the luster of good timing. We folded our clothes. Once we stood up *before* the standing vigils, *before* the popping vats, *before* the annotated lists of marshaled forces with their Venn diagrams like anxious zygotes, their paratactic chasms . . . *before* the set of whirligig blades, modular torrent. We folded our clothes. Once we remembered to get up to pee . . . and how to pee in a gleaming bowl . . . soaked as we were in gin and coconut, licorice water with catalpa buds, golden beet syrup in Johnny Walker Blue and a beautiful blur like August fog, cantilevered over the headlands . . . We tucked into the crevices of the mattress pad twirling our auburn braids, or woke up at the nick of light and practiced folding our clothes. Our pod printed headbands with hourly updates, announcing the traversals of green-shouldered hawks through the downtown loop, of gillyfish threading the north canals, of the discovery of electron calligraphy or a new method of washing brine. We smoothed our feathers like birds do, and twitched ourselves into warm heaps, and followed the fourth hand on the platinum clocks sweeping in arcs from left to right, up and down, in and out . . . We were steeped in watchfulness, fully suspended, itinerant floaters—ocean of air—among the ozone lily pads and imbrex domes, the busting thickets of nutmeg, and geode malls. At night we told stories about the future with clairvoyant certainty. Our clothing was spectacular and fit to a T. We admired each other with ferocity.

UNCONTAINABLE

As morning settled she watched the petal of the overblown lily—orange cream—fall like a fledgling—snatched by the small thicket of ferns—and simmer there. She saw light scroll across the floor, transform the splatter pattern from blue to near-white, and white walls kneading blue out of their shadows. She watched from her chair as she had learned to do, gasping at each shift of color and line—vamping materium—shedding contour and fill—retooled her own sense of purpose and form—crackling in her thorax or rustling in her spine—as if her inner membranes had been pricked and the soft tissue torn free and some amoebic assonance transferred her to this bath of objects in transition . . . She bowed to the charity of light in her corner as her conversions spread she fed on slatted chairs more slatted, pleated drapes more deeply creased . . . red cushions gushing . . . and now the uncontainable lilies as though she'd bridled at tedious common sense and in a spew let fly her own . . . curling jet . . . her backflip aurora . . . her upward peeling splash, sprung lunge *scintille* . . . she shuddered and shook with each iteration in the elemental room she occupied in the middle of May . . . apricot eucharist spillover *jeté*. . . !

AGAIN

We tug at our shirttails (down) and belt loops (up)—gravity's analog—and test the wind with our index fingers pointed to Halifax. We say goodbye to the silent peaks that scorched our dreams—North Periscope and Dry Forever—nod to the scattered bones of the house, portentous like snakes in shade—to snatch an image from the air in 3D and give it steel walls, parquet floor!—and wrap the dried crab strips and oleander gum in parchment tubes we brought from Egypt—our pageant is an atlas—singing travel songs in the basso register only the saddleback tortoises can hear, with their primal somnolence and kettle-drum hides, stone hierophants . . . Invades like the morning chill; sweeps the sky like a falling tail section; cleaves the ground like quake boots, iron cleats . . . We have to go and we wanted to go; we needed a change and we were asked to change; we were heaved out and we broke the door down. Together we crack black walnuts and read the telltale folds . . . a continuous ripple of participatory discourse . . . plenitude and solitude . . . the walking stick's resplendent calm . . . to be still in motion, to waver in measure, to center the matrix as it reels . . . with our water helmets and glistening sun cuffs fitted . . . we disable the iris keys and thumbprint codes, powder the threshold and set the ibex free to roam the crag . . . snap the hatch closed . . . in the back seat by the back window—head in the nest of my hands—I watch the dust rise, the jimson weeds slide by, the crystal towers jostle and shift, the ruts unroll . . .

THE ADVENTURE

Thumbing through the miscellany—divination clatter—with its Holstein cows like calico hills, its bluebell swards and anthracite bluffs, its hidden holding pens with blood-streaked floors . . . I forged ahead, zealously kicking snowballs and gumballs, jumping ravines, leaping rivers, *to where the beautiful nights dance like bears* and spring jets rise to lubricate the skies—clarified mind—veined by horizon lines . . . Take the tissue of this day, our cloak of torpor burst like roe—wild fennel on the air-stream—take the crackle in the sphere, black mint of creosote, the tiny flycatcher's whizz-by flame . . . Here are tins of jellyfish curd we made when we got up and brushed our chestnut hair, and creased our pleated skirts and pants and pinched our cheeks to raise the pink—laid out on placemats with our scribbled names like string pulls . . . conjure wands . . . In a huddle on a blanket at the edge of the city we watch the pale hemisphere shake off airplanes, blinking satellites, whirring insects fat as grapes, cloud ribbons writing code . . . we rouse together . . . breathe in as if floating . . . out as if flying . . . the slow tonal total hemisphere open . . . and distance . . .

from FLOWERS & SKY

HE STOOD

He stamped his feet and opened the door, stood on the threshold, turned around. The desert light shrank his eyes, sun slammed his face—he almost lost his breath—blond shiny grasses, ring of distant mountains pinking in the haze, the scorched but somehow fertile earth—he wiped his brow—he couldn't go in, he couldn't move, he couldn't say why—as if he too were a thing dried in sunlight, stopped in his tracks in the heat that fixed him in its gaze—rattlesnake Medusa—where he breathed the stinging dusty winds as though a rock inhaling rock—his proper evolution?—and fed on silence as it flowered and fell—the fierce clarity, the fierce restraint—front door behind him hanging open like a thrown shadow as he blazed in place . . . a man *inside* the view . . . the zooming arc . . . and edge to edge the blue absolute . . .

STILL WALKING

Look at the sky: it reeks of projection. Look at my eyes: they're tools of the sky. Look at my feet: still walking. *"Which way are you walking?"* Ask the birds. *"What are you singing?"* A walk-along song. "How does it go?" Bird, dome, pink, breeze . . . // mind-light in the alphabet trees . . . And more like that . . . Look at my smile: it goes up to the right. Is that my sly inflection, a mark of selection, the pitch of glory, the angle of erection? *"All that, but rhymier."* I watched a man who bought a bouquet; pleasure made him wiggle as he walked away. He swished unawares; the peonies winked and smiled to the right. *"What was he singing?"* A wiggling song. *"How did it go?"* Back and forth. *"Ah, the world's a stage."* Look at the page.

SONG

His light, his *light*, from off his face—or was it in his face? Like that shiny planet of the mind that is *in* my sky. He's my sky for today. *His* light, his *light*, which is *my* light in my mind . . . Is he *in* my face, are my eyes his sky? He was near translucent after psychedelics when I saw him, was it *my* high, am I now translucent . . . ? *His* light, his *light*, coming through me, when I saw him on the corner as the breeze blew from the sky-within or the sky-without like the birds sing in the bird-trees . . . *My* planet that he made today with his eye- and his skin- and his sky-light . . . *His* light, his *light* . . . !

from THE BLUE ABSOLUTE

ONCE...

Once I was a sailor in a fiction of the sea for a made-up self on a boat of text . . . I was happy as a comma when the waves broke, lifting me like a magic carpet into the changeable mist, then driving me down through the indigo gulf on a slant of ablutions, erasure. And what of the mist with its long gray hair and crystal kiss—a little template of the fallen sky, thickened for disappearing acts—what of its rolling folds, rich as a bisque, seething like a surname or a lexicon well? And what of the gulf and its plot-driven plunge, its quicksilver slippages—darting eels—and leading clues of bluey holes, descending . . . ? Once I was or could have been or may yet be a magnificent sailor, spelled out on a graph of azure rills, with hologram eyes that tell of spillover holds or vanishing dives or shedding selves . . . I bob in the chop, wail in the spray, plunder the swells . . . And what of the "was" with its cargo of facts; what of the "once" with its blown-open hatch . . . and flowering mast . . . and panoramic sails . . .

WE ARE SOME PLACE

We are some place that isn't now, with our bougainvillea shorts in a tangle, and the salt air fresh on our florid lips—but there are no flowers here, no viney pop-ups, no scarlet puff-balls blowing light. We are people who aren't really us, changed by the falling curtains and blocks of ice, the spasms under sheeted clouds of shrieking rain, that pocked our arms with scars like bite marks . . . cinder stars . . . How did we change so fast, dropping our books and wigs in haste, dazed by the silver ripples in the sky that seemed to know our secret wants and needs . . . ? We fell hard, wanting to be known, *hurting* to be had . . . as one by one we took the gelatin host, molded into our lungs so every breath we drew was stuck with the gum of who we couldn't be, a thickened gasp of passing phantoms . . . Shaking our heads, arms hacking the air, we fled—but how do you flee the sky?—we stopped—or were we commanded to stop?—we settled—is that the term for falling down?—forever restless in our toes and lobes, heavy to sit and light to think. We are happening sometime that isn't where we are, in a seam of a seal we can't remember or describe . . . and pace the quadrant up and down, and claw the ether as if it were fitted stone, and glance over our shoulders in nervous twists as if we were coming to get ourselves, pale and driven and blazoned with revenge . . .

MADE A SONG

Floating up and walked along and made a song: "Little Buddha in the clouds, squat upon the rise, what is the prize?" And thus, "Oh great woman on the lowland chair—anything is fair . . . " She thought, "Nah, where's the fair in that?" and walked some more . . . Woman, Buddha, cloud, chair, floating, walking shadows in the higher air: as I look, screen, worry, dream, work, speak, under your sign of my projection—though high—I bow—to find the particle unseen and bring it home into the sky, my guide . . . So I skip and crawl, puppet of the Mother Air moving puppets in the other air. This is where I dance, where I sit, what I saw and see, as given to me—or look, I can tear up space, tear up the clouds, the Buddha riding on an ozone wheel, free them all, feed them to the book—which always asks for more—tear up the book, feed it to the song, feed *all* to *all* . . . and walk some more . . .

CIRCUMFERENCE

What I came for, what I wanted to do, what I thought could be done . . . What was needed, what I was called to do . . . Who called me? Who was measuring change? What was history's name? How did it sound . . . ? Where did I land? Is this the place of rest? Is this a place of action? Did we come together or did I arrive alone . . . ? What I saw in the view, how I parsed the angles and read the stone, how I circled and came back, how I leaned out into the air as if I could smell the news, and squinted to read the scrawling clouds, and grazed my fingertips over the balcony rail to feel the shudder of the wind or the foundation shift, the axis tilt . . . What was the name of the hour I loved, when the water-jug man in the hoop of his rounds sang out the brand of his bottle named for the sky as he climbed the echoing streets, how I stayed in bed in the cool of the call and the heat of your back nestled into my chest . . . What was your name, was it echo or sky? Whose call did you hear? Were you measuring the nights? Did you parse their breathing arcs and read their rise and fall like code . . . ? What was my horizon, how did I know to turn my head? What I said and what I wrote and how I bent and how the light tore through, and how it falls, in widening circles . . . Where I landed . . . What I came for . . . Where I was called . . .

DUET

A bird, a breeze, a tease in time, a rhyme . . . A ball gown drifting down, a falling cloud or giant leaf against the sky, a light-balloon and how she watched it soar, like writing in the sky, or like a door of text . . . She opened it and fed the dream in time so that the door dreamed no end to time . . . I watched her watch, and watching rose like a bird higher than I knew to fly as if I were a cloud of feathers stung by light, and wheeled in loop-de-loops like an alphabet, she thought, a breeze of words teasing out the substance of the sky. I caught her eye in time to see the rhyme as eye to eye we rose, and smiled to be so high and high alike, and rock the light among the feathered words, and fill the sky . . .

THE THING I WAS

Once or twice I was a sailor, three times, four times, five . . . I said I was or said to be a sailor or a sail or the wind streaking or a sleek hollow hull skimming the rolling waves or the waves . . . What if the wind tore at my back to strip the canvas from the wood, free the oars, cleave the ribs, what if the sea was just a paper view, a fold of sky on a crease of blue . . . ? What if the diagram of stars, the spray, the bounding zeal were what I was told or what I told, pure air, once or twice or ten in the ear and out again, a swinging door . . . and what if the telling stopped, the alphabet unspooled, the leather notebook closed with a snap, done, and, sailor, that was that...? Well, I said, or it was said, once I was a . . . thing . . . moving over a great . . . thing... I felt the forward pull of something swift, keen as an arrow, clean as a slice . . . The . . . thing . . . I was slid across the day, skimmed the night . . . and once or again my long hair was flying, flying . . .

A MEASURE OF LIGHT

Blazoned with love as a measure of light at the city beach where the wind blows as if on the tongues of the walking men while the spangled water which is my eyes in their glee refreshes the light and the water and the men who are my glee . . . And the families are eating where the shade of the high-leafed maple falls as though sound were muffled of the singing light or the gulls in their hot shrieks who are my tongue as it measures my love and the sun swells in its lowering heat . . . There is summer in the throng in their parti-colored shorts and the orange umbrella and the ambling men with their too-big smiles and too-tight tees as they walk in that way with their hips slung low as though riding the ground that is almost the slither of their low-seated love . . . Wild slow wide day . . . and the herons amassing in a blue cloud with their legs flung behind them in glee which is summer suspended in the long low day as the blue cloud sails . . .

TURNING

Or the colors, I tell you, that the leaves pulled from the sky . . . As they fell, if they fell, if falling is flying . . . As we gasped, if we gasped, if gasping is breathing . . . and that gold, we both thought, or yellow ignited or sun strokes fired of leaves bigger than our heads—on the corner where they hung from the trees in drapes as though lit from within, it seemed, or we were, I guess, by the bright drifts we stomped through and sailed on if sailing is looking and looking. It was three days of crimson rebellion and orange confetti on the wing . . . While the sky beamed to have shot such high glitter from its great wide smile or I did or you did as we talked as we walked, if talking is drifting and walking is melting into the sky's wide smile . . .

BELIEVER

He wanted to wander; he wanted to get lost; he wanted to fuck up and get found; he wanted to fly backwards—on a broomstick in reverse—until the cooked and the raw came together . . . *under the jacaranda* she would say as if it were a myth of sound . . . He made up a place a town a day in sunlight and went there; the mountain was real as it looked down on him inventing himself in the gleam. *Madrugada* she'd say as if they were bathing in a river . . . For sure he watched the buildings fill in the heat, infused with pastel blues and pinks deepening by the hour, till noon overflowed its banks—and then the thick, extracted, steaming sheen laid down to seal the houses in their painted skins . . . Yes, someone speaks to make a person in the blank space of the vista where the sky melts. Who listens, watches, springs—like a bird veering south—"a light in sound, a sound-like power in light" high in the stream—for the pure angle of inception, the inscrutable edge of flight—believer—and the company of wings . . .

SHIVER

for San Francisco

I. GREEN EYES

Now what I saw was the same but my eyes were different, turned green like my mother's immediately after she died. How did she die? Incrementally. Long gone now ago in some space, historical, as though stretched thinner towards air . . .

And me too pulled into threads, or you in your smoke drift who have come so far to read the clouds and stars in their formation on a page . . . He remembers corn dogs and bulldogs, dreamsicles and ventricles, leather belts that whistled

and struck, and cabbage soup to soothe the hiss and the strike. Not in sequence but stacked like plates and conflated . . . And those pinwheel clocks spinning forward and back. A boy is a prelude, then an afterthought, then a molten core . . .

He armed himself with elocution and adorned himself with pride. Like a thief in plain sight he stole gender from the fem-bots and dude-droids, layered his body with faux leather and faux lace, muslin printed with snake sigils,

and saris of indigo denim fit for a wrangler—one with bangles big as cow eyes, that is, lighthouse beams that swept in widening arcs as he twirled, to flame the countryside like a dragon, set the village ablaze as the dragon in drag

he was, on fire, or so the cops thought when they stopped him for flying without a leash and buried his head in their waist-handy hood, by which I retired into the ground with a groan of lavender fumes, which will henceforth be my subtitle

when they exhume me in my marble book. Yes I talk as if I lived, but the fiction of me is merely your pleasure in deconstructing the violent world, so I dance with arms akimbo in an interrogative stance, and sing out of tune

as I do for a music of bent aspirations and uncommon grace. You remember that drinking fountain you led him to, and tipped his face into the black water so he could taste the poison syrup in its full splendor, fragrant as burning shame,

with a nose of infallible encyclicals and notes of medieval edicts tacked to stone walls? Yes, he carried that spice to make the man inside him thirsty for good, un-slaked, with a tongue for negative capability and lips formed to

suck the juice from the bones he raised. Where did the sky come in? When did it sever the present from the past and eat the human terms, the diminutives and endearments? How did the blue start to glow in our hands and bloom in our faces as we shed our scales, how did the new skin bristle like parchment as we spoke to each other in welts and rashes the new text of the new alphabet of the new history . . . ? If I say "the past" I mean my mother.

If I say "my mother" I mean the boy I was. If I say "I was" I mean something was here condensed from the air with a specific gravity you hung a name on—if that was you hanging names under the eucalyptus leaves in the rain.

I hang on your every word as the city shivers, words like "mortgage," my beloved, and "high-rise," my evil twin. The city shivers. The city shivers. Now what I saw was not the same but my green eyes . . . my mother shivers . . .

my green eyes . . . He remembers how you tasted bathed in his sweat, he remembers how you tasted roasted in his juices, your nipples spurting and your hips flexed on his incline, how could he not remember, an ocean more, more wet,

more rushing, more swells, more salt, of that contribution the verses are written in shivers . . . my green eyes . . . remember . . . And the story about two men in kilts or culottes, the story of two women in jackboots and capes, of four men

and six men and ten men who shivered in silver streetlight in contraband rain in communal moonlight till morning shot the city with frost or glitter now the city doesn't shiver . . . The city doesn't shiver. In Part II I discover the cure for allegiance. In Part Seven I dismantle the binary system as a scam of chiaroscuro for the rainbow impaired. He drank his coffee—elixir of measure—at the sidewalk café, dodging belt-bombs and snipers defending their tables

or standing on chairs in an ambush of lectures on right thinking, right acting, right killing, right versing and if in the end he was beheaded for forgery or failing to inspire his green eyes no longer remember . . . but time slowed

as my mother receded into that space where vectors converging unravel like a knot in my heart loosened or hers under surgeon's thread pulsing free, an explosion of sorts, and flowed onward . . . The city shivers. That was my home

you sold, my golden nest, my chamber of solace, my secret place of rest, that was my chair for age and my couch for sleep and my desk for sleeplessness and my rug for bedazzlement, that was my work you sold that framed

the walls as if they lived like eyes, green as the lunging trees outside, the city the city the city shivers. Do you remember that hilltop above the hilltops where light fell like water to drench our wide-open faces and the whole thing

spread out before us coast to Bay, rise and fall, as we locked hands to seize and store the image and our lingering kiss drew in the streets and parks and timbered houses and raw incendiary sky as if kissing were breathing, still breathing, pressed together as one inhalation, the city inside us, rise and fall . . . my mother breathes . . . her green eyes . . . open wide, my same eyes . . . open wide. The city . . . shivers, its green eyes . . . breathe . . .

II. HOUSE OF AIR

How does time with its hammer and tongs . . . so that invisible . . . the past invisible . . . *House of Air*, he said . . . He was climbing a wooded trail, which may have been a dream or a vision, as if climbing itself were an ark to the visible,

and the red, slick madrones, the twisty manzanita shrubs, clawed through the time or the fog or the curtain of air and refused to back down—surveyors or sentinels—inviolable—rooted in the rank . . .

Would you bring me back if you could, would you strip the mausoleum to see my happy face again, with its echoing eye-sockets and omni-grinning jaw, would you dust me off, blow out my nostrils, fit me with lips of pearl

to revisit our nacreous kisses, slick as oysters and silver-blue as their shells . . . ? invisible kisses . . . How does time with its hockey stick, its crack of polished wood . . . ? Would you call me back to feed on your prime . . . ?

She is back at her desk, that sifting machine . . . She is caught framed in the window by a passing gull. She sees what she sees, though what proof is that? Against the wall of books—shelves of Honduras pine—her silhouette flayed by the blinds, she lists in sequence the towns burned, the cities under water, what she remembers and what she's been told, what she's read in The Book of Slaughter and The Book of Stains, The Codex of Compton,

and the Index of Vanishing Holes, her sifting machine chuffing like an engine as her hand moves like a wand . . . invisible grief . . . in the House of Air . . . on a Thursday afternoon . . . as though living inside a ravenous scroll

that lengthens as she reads, of which she is the author or the scribe she can't tell, and runs her fingers through her hair to slow down the march of time so she can breathe . . . she breathes . . . and time slows . . . and time slows . . .

Once I was a sailor when the sky was one thing, a blue breath from pole to pole I caught in my wild hair and out-flung hands as if *I* were the boat I sailed, and streamed on the gleam off the waves to any place I named . . .

Once under the unified sky that blew itself in gusts of blue that filled his mouth with air that took the shape of names he shouted, and banked into the wild verses that claimed the places he needed to be or go—invisible vision—

by which he traveled to himself and back in a blue cocoon of voices as if he were the sail, the boat, the sky, the wind, the mounting waves and rushing air, the place he wanted to see, the person he wanted to be, he was, once, when, a sailor.

Take her hand as she parts her hair and wipes her brow. Is it a butterfly of thought? Remember what she can't forget. The children with their eyes like dinner plates, the wiggling dog, the imprint on the mattress

and its shape of smells—invisible ardor—How does time with its shovel, its iron clang . . . ? She adds your name to the list. She won't forget you, visitor, denizen, prisoner, supplicant, émigré, traveler, stopping by this house of air . . .

III. BREATHE

My green eyes floating in the dark . . . And breathed as if the sky were sitting on my lungs. It has to be communal. It has to be beyond remembering or forgetting. The pages need to rustle and turn by themselves,

as if the wind of the arriving news were blowing from start to finish, front to back . . . Invisible book . . . My mother reads, her green eyes peel back the letters . . . And then he just seemed to come apart in his limbs,

like a marionette with strings snipped—and would've fallen to the ground were he not already scraping the ground—his eyes with their retinas lifting away in shock—and the floaters zooming in like drones of the vitreous . . .

Invisible vision . . . now, yes, but behind the steel mounds, the hubs of digital clouds or digital air or electric packets delivering shivering sums of shivering sums, the city denuded, the hills leveled and the valleys filled in . . .

He sold his pillow for $5k . . . It has to be collective, it has to be grabbed by the throat and shaken . . . or was that you shaking me out of slumber, as I woke to clouds of plaster dust circling the room like a tiger, the bricks and timber shattered in the cold . . . the city shivering . . . Which was the real history? Was there more than one? One behind another behind another . . . Who arrived, who left, who stayed against all odds . . . ? Who danced on the tabletops

in a flurry of pastel scarves and three-day stubble squealing, "*spaciousssssss*," and built a theatre out of Kleenex boxes and nail polish for a musical version of *Long Day's Journey into Night*—in Pig Latin!—and brought the house down;

or sailed away on the barques of the epidemic from Laredo to ruin with a smile that wouldn't fade and a free pass to a convo with the angels; or got priced out, evicted, and laid off all at once but was saved by her business

of hand-made organic shrouds, no irony . . . one behind another, not in sequence but stacked like plates and conflated. If I say "I remember," does that mean I made it up? If I say "made it up" was history my evil twin? If I say "history"

I mean I dreamed something sifted and resifted stayed in the bottom of the pan . . . It has to be cooperative like the wind and the sail . . . As if time with its telescope or microscope she couldn't tell . . . slowed in the distance

and slowed in the foreground and her hand slowed too as the list lengthened . . . I remember . . . I made it up . . . Invisible images . . . Everyone breathe . . . Once, in the early years, he married the city, on a jagged outcrop on top of a hill with his eyes clear and the air clear and that blue-jewel horizon and his pledge of intent with his heart clear in his deep-breathing chest I take you, he said, and that clarity, that northern light, which made everything visible all at once,

with no clouds no smog no shiver no shock every cornice and balustrade, every cedar and pine, every dizzying hill and dune and tower and scalloped beach at the western edge, with the green eyes of my mother, the painter,

growing into mine, and time wide open as though stopped or unending—I do—and the covenant like a poem wide open and unending . . . Invisible innocence . . . and the joy of the wind . . . Everyone breathe . . . The city

behind the city . . . You were there, I remember, with your velvet tunic embroidered with leaves (I coveted) and your straw hair in a ponytail and a gentle smile on half your face while the other half courted a lascivious leer,

and both touched me in my hard place . . . the city shivers . . . I think we walked all day and talked nonstop for hours till midnight stopped our chatter and my bed swallowed us like a lotus closing and did we wake?

Did that bed ever disgorge us? History is a vision of a version. It has to be a collaboration, it has to be stopped and started in the joy of the wind. My mother shivers . . . She remembers the fierce clarity of light . . . It shows what it needed to show, so she paints what she needs to see. I saw you from a distance: scriptural, and from close up: devotional, and from inside: sacramental. I may have made you up out of necessity. That was my home

they sold . . . Everything shivers . . . he said, "I do . . ." The sky can tell the difference between what's in front and what's behind . . . My green eyes . . . Still kissing in the blue blue light . . . One behind another . . . Everyone breathe . . .

IV. FLIGHT

Is it an elegy? Was it made up in a sigh of the wind? She checks her barometer as the scroll flaps like a flag . . . She writes as if in a trance, twisted by the torque of plate stacked over plate: a litany of migrations, displacements,

evictions, and lockouts, of monoliths tilting, and falling blockades of shade . . . her boxes full of flattened faces and the string of names rising like smoke. They inspected the floor, the foundation, the walls, the sheetrock

and bedrock, the doorjamb, the beams, but the fissure was in the vision . . . invisible vision . . . My green eyes burn. I remember the joy of the torque of the wind, with my hair flying and my blue tunic in full wingspan

and my arms locked in numberless interlocked arms and the streets slick with dew at any hour . . . Everyone breathing . . . Was paradise my evil twin? Did it tar the future with the past—invisible shadow—and draw down

the lumbering sky? Now yes, but the sky behind the sky! I remember . . . We made it up . . . He looks around him in a stupor in the corner of his small room on the bentwood chair he clings to in perpetual quake . . .

shivering in the temblor of rent-times-twelve . . . and calculates the holes that will land him in her Book of Voids—as she follows her own shivering hand, alive like a slithering cat stalking the last page. When he remembers,

his eyes begin to clear, her hand pauses mid-phrase. If he remembers, the sky jacks up. Is forgetting my evil twin? If I say "him," does history let me in? One after another as my mother watches from her hospital bed

still smiling in full sail as she breathes forward and the future forms in her green eyes . . . It has to be weathered arm in arm. It has to be made-up and put into action and released into the wild. The city shivers in my twitching eyes.

Is it anticipation or regret? I think we never got out of bed, never should, never will, and the warmth remains. I think the scent of common purpose lingers like a map of silver dew. One summer day under full sail he stood high up

on a cliff top at Land's End—ocean's edge—where the pelicans in their pterodactyl way formed themselves out of the visible distance in a forward line, and flew right by him eye level . . . face to face—their leathery grit

and bony grace . . . and kept coming single file as if made up by the sky—emissaries or remnants—with their ancient topaz eyes set for primordial crossings . . . alert to his but fixed further in common purpose . . .

and the green eyes of the great golden bridge watching . . . and the thrill of the wind . . . one by one behind another they flew so close to my high-cliff perch I seemed to fly with them, into their visible distance with the old city

high inside me as though breathing me into the future in my own now-prehistoric skin and bright purposes—I do—and the pelicans making me up in perpetual migration on a forward wing . . . invisible horizon . . .

and time slowed or the sky slowed or the wind went still and the cities merged as my mother's eyes saw what they needed to see . . . the city *in* the city . . . still kissing in blue light . . . He settles his breath to steady his hand,

sings a song he thought was a dirge but may be a lullaby for the newborn—take my hand or wing—It has to be locked arm in arm, flung in formation out of the hole in sky . . . The city quivers . . . It has to be made . . . It has to be made . . .

V. SHAKE

A shiver is a rip in time. He puts his ear to the ground where the deep magma sings. History is a version of the future, a sweep of pterodactyl wings in rising light . . . The pavement quivers like jelly but doesn't split as the hot steam

vents . . . The future is underground: the city beneath the city. It has to be endured while the crippled buildings sway, molded when still hot, sculpted in the thrill of the wind . . . She watches from a distance, waiting for the ink to dry,

hand raised high in the air as if trying to escape the pull of the page . . . She wants a new sheet clear as an alien sky, blue-white and tight right to the edges. And Boom! It was like someone had dropped a piano on the floor above me—

more a thud than a shake—except I lived on the top floor, no one above. Then a groan as though something trapped below wanted to get out/get in . . . The house shivered and shook. If I say "open" is hot lava my evil twin?

With his night-vision goggles—green eyes—he looks for every crack in time, every seam about to slip, every hollow and hole—to let the old city roar in and wake the sleeping walking un-looking pixel-bound dead . . .

Where is the sky now? Does it pulse like an organism, does it breathe in silver waves and tremble like morning dew? The sky beneath the sky! And you with your long hair like strands of fire—I think we burned up that bed—

I think we live in those flames, still burn—I think our kisses are comets in the shivering sky . . . And in the hot silence of the blank streets he walks as if in a trance, with time stretched and stacked like plates, and my mother's eyes

squinting to keep the plates conflated—invisible gravity—while the temblors rock his footsteps and the wooden houses squeal in their beautiful joints and the violins of the tall cedars wail their ache and awe . . . up the steep hill

behind his house where the downtown towers seem already pitched forward, ready to fall, and the far-out Pacific racing in—green eyes of the deep water where the bones of the buildings lay . . . the city quivers . . . now, but before

the great shiver . . . He buries his face in his cupped hands as if submerged in deep water, holding his breath to stop time and lock in the memories—her raised arm aching but desperate to live the pause, to hold back the footnotes

on tent cities, tossed syringes, immune deficiencies—and release the city from its litany of litanies . . . He spins in place to keep his balance and ride out the shake—history is a whirlpool from which only the spinners wake—

in common purpose out of a hole in the sea—I remember—hot lava made me . . . What did they see? What did they know? How did they work? How did they work together? Who did they want to be? Who did they become?

How many had green eyes? How many loved history? Whose mother's heart blew apart its sutures in a last attempt to keep the ways in play . . . ? Once I fell to the floor in my little house in a skylight beam of almost solid sun

and lay my cheek on the bamboo planks in a pose of surrender and a shiver of thanks . . . Once we climbed the distant mountain in the eastern county after big rain with the thick mud congealing around our shoes like bear traps,

locking our steps . . . Still we trudged on, mud-bound, not for the summit per se but just to see from the top the city across the bay shining in its sheath of western light, with the glamorous fog like a sequined cape on its shoulders

jeweling the shadows—"sunset couturier"—and the red-tinted hawks wheeling in a vortex of suspended breathing . . . the city shimmers . . . Once in a park in a cool breeze with my notebook un-sutured in my lap

I watched the hummingbirds in their mating dance climb the air out of sight then plummet straight down on an axis of love in flight—flickers of red and green in a daredevil swerve of light . . . Once I met a man in a bar . . . Once I met a man at a café . . . Once I met a man in the drugstore up and down the shadowy aisles . . . Once I met a man and once I met a man . . . I do . . . and rode the wind in my sheets to make our bodies shiver on an axis of love in flight . . . I remember

like it was tomorrow . . . Which city through the tumbling night? Long long ago he would ride the late late bus into the city with his eyes not yet green but pressed like suckers to the window glass to see the spires lit up as if on fire

with his heart lit up as if on fire and the hot lava of his blood . . . and he seemed to pitch and stagger through the late streets on the quaking jolts of the city under the city—tossed around in the torque of desire that would unmake him

and make the city his—indivisible citizen—arm in arm hand in hand—I do—How we take the brilliant northern light and . . . how we face the monstrous towers in their sky of shade to . . . how you grab my hand so we can . . .

how we inhale together on a silver wave of . . . how our notebooks tremble with their diagrams of . . . how he bends to kiss his mother's forehead just to . . . how his green eyes slice through traffic, mammoth buses, lonely shopping carts so . . .

how she lays down her pen and closes the book and walks out the door for . . . how we gather in the plaza and thread each other's eyes on a pledge of intent to . . . how we tack a notice to the door for . . . how we close our eyes to dream and open our eyes to dream . . . on the lip of the western edge . . . How I bear down into the stacked worlds where my now-green eyes gleam, and parse the realms and track the turns and scan the prepositions—*behind*, *in*, *under*—

to meet the city that made me and that I make—by wing or by shoulder, on an axis of love in flight—one behind another inside another beneath another . . . with the sky pulsing, molten . . . and the city breathing in the blue blue light . . .

INDEX TO POEM TITLES

BIBLIOGRAPHY

The Night Sun. San Francisco: Gay Sunshine Press, 1976.

Giving up the Ghost. San Francisco: Rose Deeprose Press, 1980.

The Graces. San Francisco: Four Seasons Foundation, 1983.

A's Dream. Oakland: O Books, 1989.

Into Distances. Los Angeles: Sun & Moon Press, 1993.

Unbound: A Book of AIDS. Los Angeles: Sun & Moon Press, 1997.

The Paradise of Forms. Jersey City: Talisman House, 1999.

A Door. Jersey City: Talisman House, 2000.

Involuntary Lyrics. Richmond: Omnidawn Publishing, 2005.

Citizen. San Francisco: City Lights Books, 2012.

Flowers & Sky: Two Talks. Seattle: Entre Ríos Books, 2017.

The Blue Absolute. New York: Nightboat Books, 2020.

AARON SHURIN is the author of fourteen books of poetry and prose. He has been a central member of the San Francisco Bay Area writing community for half a century, having taught a generation of poets at universities throughout the city. A graduate himself of the storied Poetics Program at the New College of California, he is a professor emeritus and former director of the MFA Writing Program at the University of San Francisco. Shurin has been a pioneer in both LGBTQ studies and in contemporary innovative poetry, challenging fixed notions of gender and sexual identity, lyricism and narrativity, and the structure of verse. For forty years, in language at once lush and colloquial, he has spearheaded the resurgence of the prose poem as a crucial form of modern art.

NIGHTBOAT BOOKS

Nightboat Books, a nonprofit organization, seeks to develop audiences for writers whose work resists convention and transcends boundaries. We publish books rich with poignancy, intelligence, and risk. Please visit nightboat.org to learn about our titles and how you can support our future publications.

The following individuals have supported the publication of this book. We thank them for their generosity and commitment to the mission of Nightboat Books:

Kazim Ali, Anonymous (4), Ava Aviva Avnisan, Jean C. Ballantyne, Will Blythe, V. Shannon Clyne, Theodore Cornwell, Ulla Dydo Charitable Fund, Gisela Gamper, Photios Giovanis, Amanda Greenberger, David Groff, Parag Rajendra Khandhar, Katy Lederer, Shari Leinwand, Elizabeth Madans, Ricardo Maldonado, Ethan Mitchell, Caren Motika, Elizabeth Motika, Asker Saeed, The Leslie Scalapino - O Books Fund, Amy Scholder, Thomas Shardlow, Benjamin Taylor, Jerrie Whitfield & Richard Motika, Clay Williams

This book is made possible, in part, by grants from the New York City Department of Cultural Affairs in partnership with the City Council, the New York State Council on the Arts Literature Program, and the Topanga Fund, which is dedicated to promoting the arts and literature of California.